M000189123

940.354092
H9391

Hunt, Antonia
Little resistance...

35842

M

DEMCO

SQUALICUM HS LIBRARY

T 48927

LITTLE RESISTANCE

A Teenage English Girl's Adventures in Occupied France

ANTONIA HUNT

BELLINGHAM HIGH SCHOOL LIBRARY

35842

St. Martin's Press
New York

940.54092
H 939 l

LITTLE RESISTANCE. Copyright © 1982 by Antonia Hunt. All
rights reserved. Printed in the United States of America. No
part of this book may be used or reproduced in any manner
whatsoever without written permission except in the case of
brief quotations embodied in critical articles or reviews. For
information, address St. Martin's Press, 175 Fifth Avenue, New
York, N.Y. 10010.

Library of Congress Cataloging in Publication Data

Hunt, Antonia.
    Little resistance.

    1. World War, 1939-1945—France.   2. Hunt, Antonia.
3. World War, 1939-1945—Personal narratives, English.
4. World War, 1939-1945—Prisoners and prisons, German.
5. France—History—German occupation, 1940-1945.
6. Children—England—Biography.   7. Children—France
—Biography.   8. Prisoners of war—Great Britain—
Biography.   9. Prisoners of war—France—Biography.
I. Title.
D802.F8H86   940.53'161   82-5730
ISBN 0-312-48866-1   AACR2

First published in Great Britain by Leo Cooper in association
with Martin Secker & Warburg Ltd.

First U.S. Edition

10 9 8 7 6 5 4 3 2 1

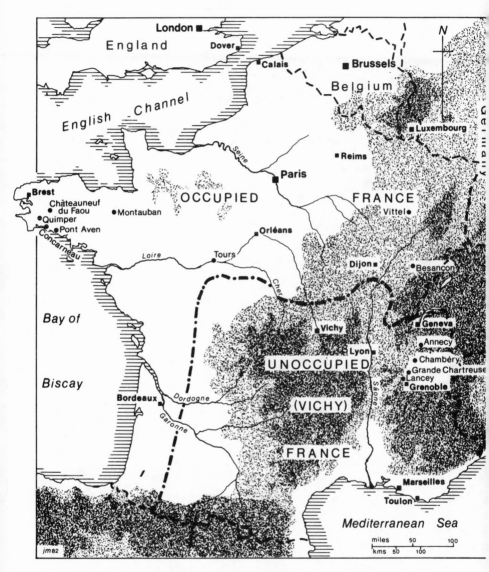

France, showing occupied and unoccupied zones.

I

☙ Prelude ❧

I WAS AN only child. My father, Tristram Lyon-Smith, was a regular officer in the Royal Horse Artillery. My mother was Canadian. They were devoted to each other. At the time of my birth my father was stationed in India and they travelled to Canada on leave so that I could be born there. Two months later my mother rejoined my father in India. I was left to spend the first two years of my life at Strathallan on Lake Simcoe, in Ontario, with my grandparents and an adoring household of aunts and uncles. When my parents returned to England I was brought over to rejoin them and a girl of seventeen was engaged to be my nanny. I loved her from the very beginning and I am glad to say we are still in close touch. She has always been an important part of my life.

When I was six we all four travelled out to Egypt where my father was to be stationed at Heliopolis for two years. As there was a risk of polio there at that time I led a secluded life, with daily lessons taught by Nanny, who doubled up as governess for those two years. In the cool of the early morning, the Egyptian groom used to take me out on my white donkey, Jill. He would run behind, whacking her gently with a stick to make her go. The lower part of the Sphinx was still being excavated and long rows of natives brought up baskets of sand from beneath her massive paws. I remember being too frightened to ride a camel, though everyone else did, including Nanny!

For two months each summer, Nanny and I used to travel to Cyprus to avoid the intense heat. We lived in a tent on a camping site on the slopes of the Troodos mountains. My parents joined us for two weeks' summer leave.

Shortly after our return to England, as I was by then eight or nine, Nanny went to Brittany in France to look after my little cousin. Her mother, Diana, was my mother's niece and had married a Frenchman and acquired French nationality. They lived in Concarneau, in a very nice house right on the sea.

Two years later my parents were again posted back to India which, they felt, would not be particularly healthy for me, now aged ten. Diana asked me to go and live with them, and so I was reunited with Nanny and had my young cousin, aged five, to play with. I spent two extremely happy years with this family, learning French with a dear old French Mademoiselle who was very strict. I used to bicycle to her house every morning and worked very hard. For six months I learnt nothing but French, becoming fluent and grammatically correct. After that, all lessons were conducted in French: maths, geography, Latin, history. This was to prove a great asset later on. During the afternoons Nanny and I and my young cousin, Micky, would take Snow, the black spaniel, for walks on the beach, or swim during the long hot summers. Looking back, it was an idyllic time, taken for granted, as children do.

When my father's posting in India ended, he and my mother returned to live at Catterick Camp in Yorkshire and I rejoined them. For the first time, aged just thirteen, I went to boarding school – and hated it!

4

There was a last summer holiday in Canada in 1938 at my grandparents' house on Lake Simcoe. My cousin's family came out too, which meant that Nanny, Micky and I were together again. The woods round the house were close to the lake and magical to play in. A long bumpy track led down to the boathouse on the lake, where we had picnics of corn-on-the-cob while Micky and I would swim naked in the clear, cold water and paddle the little canoe happily for hours.

My Grandfather – a lawyer who became a Canadian King's Counsellor – was of Jewish extraction, but not of that faith. His Father was one of the very few Jews to be made a Bishop in the Anglican Church; he was Bishop of Huron, Ontario. Their name was Hellmuth and this was to cause me more terror than anything else throughout the war.

My life until now had been sheltered and quiet. Being constantly on the move, there was little time to make friends and, after Nanny had gone to Brittany, I was alone a lot. My mother usually wrote letters in the morning and played bridge or golf most afternoons, often being joined by my father when his duties were over. I would go along as "caddy". Riding lessons were conducted by my father, an excellent horseman, but they often ended in tears! I seemed to have no hobbies except reading and day-dreaming.

In those days just before the war, living in army quarters, life seemed suspended. I never read the newspapers, seldom listened to the wireless. No one ever discussed war, politics, money, religion, sex or any "grown-up" subjects with me. I was in total ignorance of what was going on abroad.

Just before the outbreak of war we were living in quarters in Bulford Camp in Wiltshire. All officers had two magnificent horses and a groom. It is incredible to think that the eighteen-pounder guns were still being pulled by these chargers. Occasionally I was allowed out over Salisbury Plain on one of my father's horses with the groom, and one day remains a vivid and painful memory. I was riding "Bones", a huge animal, and was, in fact, on a leading rein. I felt like trying a small jump, which seemed a good idea to the groom. "Bones" soared over it – and then bolted! I was helpless. Over the plain we galloped, my only thought being "*Please*, God – don't let him put a foot down a rabbit hole and break a leg, or poor Daddy will have to pay for him." (I should explain that the horses were the property of the Army.) By some miracle I didn't fall off, and eventually the horse tired himself out. I entreated the groom not to tell anyone, mentally vowing never to ride again!

When the war was declared on 3rd September, it was just two weeks to my fourteenth birthday. I couldn't help feeling a certain excitement mixed with dread. A few days later my father's regiment was sent to France with the B.E.F. (British Expeditionary Force) and we had to vacate the army quarter, putting everything into store. Selfishly I thought only of my own few precious possessions. What would happen to my bicycle (bought with my own savings) and my beautiful doll's house? My mother's first husband had been killed in the 1914–1918 War only three months after their marriage and she adored my father, so she must have found my behaviour very trying.

We went to stay with friends. Secretly I hoped that I wouldn't have to go back to school, which I hated. I was hopeless at practically everything except French. However, when term started, back to school I went, while my mother, now having no home, tried to decide where to go and what to do. I felt dutifully sad, and important, as my father was already "fighting" the war.

Towards the middle of term my mother came to see me, having reached a decision. She told me Diana had asked her if she would like to spend the war in Brittany with her. It would mean that my father need not cross the Channel every time he came on leave. She was thinking of the 1914–1918 War, when the battles raged in France alone. Then she asked me if I would like to spend the war with my grandparents in Ontario. They would love to have me there.

For the first time in my life I was adamant. I flatly refused. I felt I couldn't bear to be out of it all, and begged her to allow me to go with her to Concarneau. I reasoned that, as I could speak French, I could go to the Lycée in Concarneau, and promised not to be a nuisance. My mother eventually agreed. If either of us had known what would happen over the next five years, would we still have taken that decision? I certainly would have.

The negotiations with authorities to obtain permission to travel to France, at a time when most people were returning from that country, were lengthy and complicated. Finally, with a trunkful of school clothes, and most of my mother's personal belongings, we left Dover for Calais in November, 1939, to cross the heavily-mined Channel. We were the only passengers in a small cargo ship, and had to wear bulky, old fashioned cork life-jackets the whole way across. Minefields had been laid as soon as war broke out, so we dodged our way across, keeping to the "safe" lanes. The lifejackets prevented one from lying down, which made sleep difficult, but the mixture of excitement and fear would have prevented it anyway. We talked in hushed voices, partly because we were frightened and partly influenced by the unreality of the dimly-lit cabin. To take my mind off it, I thought about school and how

7

wonderful it was to have escaped. Apart from the construction of a couple of air-raid shelters and some half-hearted attempts at air-raid practice and drill, the war had had little effect on life at school. Some girls would go down into the shelters and kiss each other, but I could see no point in this, having never heard of lesbianism. It may seem hard to believe, but in those days girls of fourteen were mainly innocent of any unconventional behaviour. The girls in my form had been very envious when I told them I was leaving for France. For the first time I was the centre of attention.

The crossing lasted for hours, and we were very relieved when a steward brought us some hot sweet tea and told us it was nearly over.

Calais was noisy, bustling and cheerful, quite unlike a country at war. In a tired and unreal day-dream, we collected our belongings and found our way to the Paris train. The port was full of French soldiers, all going somewhere noisily and excitedly – so different from their British counterparts who always seemed so quiet.

The journey by train from Calais to Concarneau via Paris resembled any wartime journey – trains held up because of troop movements, and a total blackout in Paris because at that early stage of the war the French expected an air-raid or an invasion at any moment. Nevertheless, the atmosphere was totally unlike the feeling in England. Perhaps the intangible, indefinable smell of Gauloises, garlic and scent had something to do with it! The French soldiers smiled and waved at all the girls – including me! It was my first taste of being treated as a woman. It was fun; and, best of all, no school or lessons for at least a week. My French, although a bit rusty after two years in England, was a help, and having lost and retrieved bits of luggage on the way, we reached the peace and quiet of Concarneau at last. My mother had visualized a repeat of the 1914–1918 War so she had packed for a four-year siege!

II

❧ Invasion ❧

IT WAS A happy reunion. The Provosts' house in Concarneau was not large but it had a lovely big room downstairs, a combined sitting-room and dining-room, where the piano was, and wide, wide windows overlooking the sea. My little room, in which I had slept during the two years I had lived there, also looked over the sea, and was next to my mother's. Cousin Diana, whose husband had already been called up and who was serving as a "*poilu*" (private soldier), was delighted to have us there to keep her company, as were Nanny⋆ and young Micky, now about eight years old. The old Breton cook and maid were still dressed in Breton costume and wore clogs. I was very fond of them both. It was fun to be able to slip down to the kitchen very early in the morning, before the rest of the house awoke and drink a mug of hot coffee, "dunking" the crisp bread and tangy Breton butter. Nothing has ever quite matched up to those stolen breakfasts.

Obviously the boring question of education had to be dealt with and, my French being quite adequate, I was provided with a bicycle and sent off to the Lycée in Concarneau.

The French system of education is very simple – *everyone* goes to the Lycée, so no one is any different from anyone else. The fisherman's sons and daughters,

---

⋆ Victoria Jeynes who now lives with her sister in Driffield, Yorkshire.

the rich industrialist's children, all mix happily together. To me, at first, in a huge classroom, with so many boys, which I wasn't used to, it seemed terrifying; especially as, in those days, all lessons were literally learnt by heart and had to be recited in class. I thought I would be laughed at. I was quite wrong. I was an anonymous drop in a friendly ocean, and *work* was the important thing. Everyone wanted to learn, wanted to do well, actually enjoyed school. Soon I did too; and very soon I had the first pangs of calf love for one of the senior boys. In breaktime (practically no games were played) excited and animated discussions went on, everyone talked at once, had so much to say, were so much more alive than the dreary girls in boarding school. I used to gaze at this incredible boy. He had very green eyes and dark curly hair – and, sadly, he never even noticed me. Still it made going to school more exciting.

That Christmas, the Christmas of 1939, my father had a fortnight's leave, and so did Diana Provost's husband. The front was quiet, and no one had any idea what might happen. Little did I imagine, during that happy fortnight that when I kissed my father goodbye, saying cheerfully, "See you at Easter, Daddy", I was not to see him again for several years.

Though we were not aware of the censorship of the French newspapers, and there were, of course, no British ones, as February slid into March our entirely feminine household became aware that all was not as it should be. The French radio was censored, and false, encouraging propaganda was churned out, but when we were unable to tune in to the B.B.C. we still thought it was bad interference or atmospherics – never dreaming it was deliberate jamming by the Germans.

For me, however, life continued normally: Lycée

every day and the weekends playing with Micky and Nanny; lovely walks along the seashore, or a trip in the car to a small peninsula called the Cabellou, which was wild in those days, and where the Provosts had a vegetable garden. On the beach at the Cabellou was a dear little house belonging to an old friend of the Provosts. Geoffroy Guichard was always very kind to me and used to tease me gently. I thought he was wonderful.

Sometimes we thought the war would be over quite soon and I selfishly dreaded the possibility of having to go back to boarding school. Mostly we were ignorant of what was going on; but the rumours were endless. Speculation increased, as did the anxiety of the two wives for their husbands. Letters became erratic and there was no leave for Daddy or for Marcel Provost. News that the Belgian Army had surrendered was dismissed as a rumour. Some British families in Brittany and elsewhere in France managed to get back to England, but until my mother had some definite news she did not want to leave.

A great cloud of anxiety hung over the Easter holidays. One felt utterly helpless, not knowing what was going on. The newspapers and wireless contradicted each other daily. The only certain fact was that the Germans had somehow avoided the Maginot Line and outflanked it.

Then came that fateful May* and for a whole month there was no word from my father – no news at all – no possible way of finding out what had happened as there was no communication between France and England. Mummy was distraught with worry for we knew now that the war was going badly. Even the newspapers admitted to battles being fought in the East of France.

---

* The German offensive began on 10th May.

"But of course, they will *never* reach Paris." That was the comforting refrain.

The weather was glorious – hot sunny days, with the sea warm enough to dash into, and, because of the war, the whole beach to one's self. The Lycée had been commandeered as a hospital for wounded soldiers, so, to my joy, there was once again no school. We spent our days playing on the beach and bathing; and the fact that there were soldiers in the town made it all incredibly romantic. Yet, beneath it all I was deeply worried, for I loved my father dearly.

At last a telegram arrived. No one knew how it had got through. It merely said that my father was back in England and that we were to join him there. The evacuation from Dunkirk was known about, though not in detail. Some French people were angry with the British for leaving them in the lurch. No one could believe that most French officers had just abandoned their men or that the Belgians had surrendered.

The next problem was how to get back to England. The only solution seemed to be to sit at any airport in Paris and pray for a seat in a 'plane. My mother reasoned, "You're perfectly safe here in Brittany – much safer than in wartime England." I agreed wholeheartedly. She went on, "Anyway, we have nowhere to live at present. When I've seen how Daddy is and where we're going to be, I'll come back for you." She also discussed it with Diana, who reassured her: "The Germans will never reach Brittany, and in any case, Tonia is safe until she's sixteen under the Geneva convention. The war will be over long before then." So we cheered ourselves through the last few days, torn between relief at Daddy's safety and doubts about flying back. Eventually Mummy gave her jewellery to Diana, saying, "Just in case anything happens to the 'plane, you look after it for me." We hugged each other goodbye, convinced it would not be for long.

She was very lucky with a flight – about the last one from Paris – and on the 'plane was a very tall young French officer. She was not aware at the time that it was De Gaulle.

Things happened fast after that. Occasionally when we turned on the wireless to listen to the B.B.C. news, a few sentences would be audible through the deliberate interference. So we knew that the Germans were definitely advancing and it wasn't long before Paris fell. The optimists were convinced the French would make a successful stand somewhere – but where and when? Petrol being unobtainable, all the shopping and vegetable-picking had to be done on a bicycle. I felt very important being allowed to bicycle the five kilometres to the Cabellou for vegtables.

A few isolated platoons of the remainder of the French Army did their best to reach England. Various ideas were thought of for me too. One or two boats did leave Brest, even at that late stage, in June, and reached England, but it was agreed by Diana and Nanny that, at fourteen, I was too young to undertake such a hazardous journey alone; so I stayed.

One day a French battalion mustered on the quayside at Concarneau and set fire to all their trucks and vehicles. They then began to embark on the tunny boats that were in the harbour, intending to sail to Bordeaux, or perhaps North Africa, to continue the fight. I was among those helping them to load their gear on board. It was a heartbreaking sight – young soldiers with practically no one to lead them, leaving on a perilous journey to nowhere in particular. I found myself looking into the sad, blue eyes of a young soldier in a tunny boat moored alongside the quay. I wished I could go with them. Their sailing kept being delayed. They needed provisions for several days and the shopkeepers in Concarneau were *giving* food away. Time after time I bicycled from the quayside to load my bicycle basket with fruit and bread and chocolate and then lowered it, on a rope, to the soldier. He flirted delightfully with me. As the boat, on the ebb tide, became lower than the quayside, he blew me kisses, and I fell madly in love with him. Night fell, and still they were there. I couldn't bear to leave. Not a word had been spoken between us, but his eyes were touchingly eloquent. Finally, at about midnight, they sailed and I waved till they were out of sight. I had never been so moved, and had certainly never stayed up so late. I cried that night. It wasn't until much later that we learnt of the sinking of all those tunny boats off Bordeaux.

More wounded soldiers kept arriving at Concarneau station. People with cars drove the mobile ones to the Hotel de Cornouaille which had also been taken over as a hospital. Bandages had been asked for, and one afternoon I was speeding along on my cousin's bicycle, taking a basketful of bandages, when I rode straight into a car. All the bandages spilled out and the front wheel was bent double. Unfortunately I wasn't hurt, so I couldn't plead for sympathy! But luckily the car was being driven by an old friend of the Provosts, who kindly took the blame on himself.

By now it was near the end of June and it didn't look as if anything could stop the Germans; but somehow it was still felt that they wouldn't bother with Finistère. The summer of 1940 was abnormally hot. The bicycle ride to the Cabellou was a hilly one and, laden with vegetables, it was a hot and dusty journey. I used to wear very short shorts and a suntop.

On what was to be my last bicycle trip to the

Cabellou, with a hot sun beating down and a heavily-laden basket of vegetables, as I rode down the hill into Concarneau I could scarcely believe my eyes. There along the quayside were massed what appeared to be hundreds upon hundreds of German tanks. They rumbled slowly along in an endless stream with the swastika flag draped over each one, and devastatingly good-looking, suntanned, blue-eyed soldiers standing up in them. I was horrified. My immediate reaction was: "How undignified to be dressed in shorts when the invasion arrives." Would they take my bike away? Would they take *me* away? As yet no one knew how they would behave. I carefully pushed my bicycle into a shop, feeling very conspicuous, as everyone had shut themselves in in order not to witness the Huns' triumphant entry into Concarneau. Then I borrowed a skirt to put over the offending shorts and carried the precious vegetables back home. The occupation had started.

The German Army behaved very correctly to start with, but the Bretons were never taken in by it. The Germans were hated and resented from the beginning. Very soon after their arrival, the requisitioning of houses and other buildings for billeting began.

Diana Provost's house was chosen by the Major in command of Concarneau. He took over the whole of the ground floor with his soldier servant. Before they moved in Diana had the piano taken upstairs, and a drawing-room was made in what had been my mother's bedroom. It seemed such a strange situation. Two English people, Nanny and me, in the same house as the actual enemy! Yvonne, the cook, and Marguerite, the maid, had to share the kitchen with the soldier servant, and gave him a very rough time. We were allowed to use the stairs and the hall to go out of the front door, but otherwise it was "out of bounds" downstairs.

I still had some friends in Concarneau – girls who were there with their parents for the summer holidays and who saw no reason to leave, as the Germans were everywhere anyway. One of them, a very sweet blonde called Nicole, was a bit older than me and we would sit in the upstairs drawing-room discussing men and playing the wind-up gramophone – the days of Jean Sablon, Charles Trenet and Edith Piaf.

When it was realized that the German's weren't going to rape everyone on sight, it was decided that to go down to the beach and swim would be safe enough. It was an extraordinary sight to see and hear large companies of German soldiers solemnly marching and singing – quite beautifully – as they paraded down to the beach. There they would don very short red swimming trunks and dash into the sea like children. None of them seemed able to swim. They never tried to molest or fraternize with anyone. After a short while in the sea a sergeant would blow a whistle, whereupon they would all rush back, sit in a circle and sing again. Their discipline had the French in fits of laughter. Nothing like it had ever been seen.

There was continuous activity up and down the coast road and on many of the beaches. They would practise landing on the beach from boats, shrieking wildly and throwing themselves on the sand. We all assumed with sinking hearts that they would soon be taking off for England and I imagined that, after the invasion, I would be able to rejoin my parents. Yet I prayed so hard that they wouldn't invade. It seemed inconceivable that the Germans should ever land in England.

Bicycling was out of the question because of the continuous movement of troops along the coast roads, but the distance across the bay to the Cabellou peninsula was not too great. Diana had a canoe and we decided to ask the German Major if I might be allowed to paddle across to bring back the desperately needed vegetables. First of all he refused flatly. Whether he imagined me canoeing to England with vital information about the troops occupying Concarneau we'll never know. It seemed too ridiculous. Nicole and I did manage to persuade him to let us take the canoe on a picnic to a nearby beach once or twice, so, when he had seen that we did come back safely, we decided to go across to the Cabellou without asking. It was further than we thought and when Nicole and I landed on the little beach just below Geoffroy Guichard's house we were hot and exhausted. We decided to have a swim and sunbathe before collecting the vegetables. We had dozed off in the hot sun when we were rudely awoken by a good-looking young sergeant with a gun. Nicole and I tried to convince him, in French, that we weren't part of a counter-invasion, but just visiting the house nearby to get food. His name was Egon Martin, he was Austrian and very friendly and helpful. He gave us permission to cross the grounds of Guichard's house in order to pick the vegetables in the Provosts' garden. Guichard had been taken prisoner, like Marcel, and I saw that they had occupied his house. I thought how dreadful it would be for him if he got back and found his house filled with Germans.

At the time it seemed quite natural to talk to the young Austrian, I was immensely attracted by him. Though only fourteen, I was tall, dark-haired and slim, with brown eyes and, of course, very sun-tanned. No one had ever commented on my appearance and I had never thought about it, except to wish I had blond curly hair and blue eyes! Unlike today's teenagers, no one of my age wore make-up in those days. I returned often to get the precious lettuce, beetroot and tomatoes, but in fact it was to see Egon. I told him I was English and had been left behind by mistake, and he told me how Austria had been forced to join Germany and fight for Hitler, for whom he had little liking . We would sit on the beach and talk and, eventually, of course, he told me I was beautiful and that he loved me. By this time I was head-over-heels in love with him and scared stiff someone would find out.

I wondered if he might do something for me as he said he loved me, so I asked him if they would leave Guichard's house and occupy someone else's, and he promised to try to arrange it. I learned much later that the Germans did, in fact, leave Guichard's house. This idyll lasted for a month or so. He kissed me – for the first time I had been kissed by a man. It was an indescribable sensation and I melted with guilty joy. Standing against the rocks on the beach he pressed his whole body against mine and in my complete ignorance and naive innocence, I wondered how wrong it was. Maybe he guessed my age, or maybe they all had strict instructions; in any case he never tried to do more. Then the inevitable happened. I was found out. The disgrace was absolute.

In the meantime all the English people over sixteen years old still living along the coast of Brittany were banished inland by the Germans. It was absurd, as only a few rather ancient couples or people like Nanny were left and they hardly constituted a serious threat to the Third Reich! Perhaps they imagined the British signalling messages across the Channel! The English were therefore sent to Châteauneuf-du-Faou, a little village in the centre of Brittany, where they were billeted in various farms and cottages. Nanny had already gone on ahead and Micky and I missed her dreadfully. Maybe I was seeking consolation by my frequent trips to the Cabellou.

The thought that Nanny might be told of my shocking behaviour plunged me into sheer misery. I cried and cried, and couldn't stop crying. Even though, being under sixteen, I didn't have to leave Concarneau, it was decided, in order to stop me seeing the young Austrian again, to send me to Châteauneuf. The seriousness of the punishment was so devastating that I couldn't help wondering if I was going to have a baby. There had only been kisses, but they had been extremely passionate!

Still, I was happy to be with Nanny again. She scolded me, of course, and pointed out how badly and unpatriotically I had behaved. She was in a very primitive farmhouse with no running water, which was provided by a massive outside pump. I was on a camp bed in her room. The first night I cried myself to sleep, but nevertheless slept soundly. The great healing gift of sleep has always stayed with me, in whatever circumstances. I'm sure that it contributed enormously to my nearly normal mental and physical health at the end of the war. My unhappiness was shortlived. There was much too much to do. There were of course no sanitary towels, so nappies had to be used, and had to be washed outside in the icy water from the pump. The outside lavatory was a hole in the ground, with two places for feet on either side. It all served as a gentle breaking-in for what was to come. The British had to sign a book every day at the police station in Châteauneuf to prove they hadn't run away! We were not allowed outside the bounds of the Parish.

My fifteenth birthday, on 20th September, was a rather sad occasion, though darling Nanny not only

20

gave me a present but managed somehow to make me a delicious cake.

For a short time school reared its ugly head again. It was arranged that I should attend the Convent in Châteauneuf. The Nuns were very kind to me and I loved wearing the wooden clogs. We all wore them, with soft slippers inside. The clogs were left by the door, and we slid our slippers into a polisher – a flat piece of felt with one strap. Thus a whole army of polishers slid across the parquet floors, which always looked marvellous. Lessons were fairly easy after Lycée work, except for sewing (not done at the Lycée). The Nuns were very keen on fine sewing. The stitches had to be tiny and neat and in complicated patterns. I soon discovered that this was yet another gift I lacked. My bit of embroidery was dirty and spotted with blood where I kept pricking my fingers, and I had many detentions for this! I had a great friend there called Andrea and we exchanged many confidences, but I never told her about my shameful conduct. She loathed the Germans as much as I did. I felt guilty for weeks and was convinced that everyone must know about it.

By now France had surrendered and Pétain had arranged his "peace with honour". The war being over for France, the French soldiers who hadn't already been released by the Germans escaped, and Marcel came home some time round then. Guichard also escaped later.

In October it was decided to meet up with the Provosts for a gargantuan dinner in Pont-Aven, and stay the night. This was tremendously exciting. One wasn't allowed to leave Châteauneuf, and not only were we doing just that, we were going near the sea, and staying away for the night! The thought of a really good meal and a comfortable night in a bed in a warm *auberge* was wonderful. The little farm cottage was freezingly cold and there was no fuel for a fire. We had to heat a kettle in order to wash ourselves or anything else. Nanny and I planned to cadge a lift in a lorry to Pont-Aven, where we would meet up with the Provosts. As we signed the book in the "commissariat" (police station), feeling guilty and wondering if it would show when we signed for two days, I never dreamt that I would never return there.

The dinner was splendid. Happiness was complete. I was forgiven and would have been in seventh heaven except that my ear kept aching on and off throughout the long and utterly satisfying meal. Nanny and I shared a room and I tried hard to sleep, but it was impossible. The pain became excruciating and forced me to cry out. I tossed from side to side, beating my head on the bed. Nanny fetched Diana and Marcel and they took my temperature. It was alarmingly high. A noise of rushing water and cascading waterfalls sounded in my ear, which made them realize I must have a burst "otite", or inner ear abscess, and would have to be operated on instantly. It was hard to stop myself from screaming. The doctor was fetched in the middle of the night and, there and then, in the auberge bedroom, he gave me an anaesthetic and operated, piercing the eardrum. When I came to, it was obvious I was very ill indeed and would have to go to hospital in Quimper for treatment. Naturally there was no penicillin in those days and my temperature was soaring. Nanny had to return to Châteauneuf, where she would have to explain my absence and above all about being in Pont-Aven when it happened. It was somehow typical of me; things happen at the wrong time.

The hospital in Quimper, the capital of Brittany, was run by nuns. Once again their gentle, patient kindness comforted me and I was extremely well looked after. My eardrum took a long time to heal over. Diana came to visit me as often as she could from Concarneau, but, as she had Micky to look after, she couldn't manage it very often. The nuns, being Roman Catholics, naturally tried hard to convert me. In their eyes, anyone not a Roman Catholic was a heathen and damned to eternal hell, so they felt very sorry for me. I couldn't make them understand that the Church of England, or Protestantism as I called it, enabled me to go to Heaven too.

The weeks passed quickly and I was soon so much better that I thought I would be able to rejoin Nanny in Châteauneuf. I was a bit lonely, in a room on my own with a few books, but no wireless.

Then one day one of the nuns fluttered in, in a great state of excitement and alarm, to tell me that a German Colonel, a doctor, was coming to see how my ear was healing. This seemed very strange to me. Why on earth should a high-ranking German take an interest in my "*otite*"? I supposed I would be ticked off for being in Quimper and would be accused of contacting England, or spying or something.

The officer came in in uniform, which seemed strangely out of place in the hospital. He sent the nun out of the room, and I felt slightly defenceless, alone in bed. I was a bit frightened, but I needn't have been. He was both courteous and reassuring. First of all he examined my ear very closely and confirmed that the eardrum had closed over and the wound healed. He then told me that he shouldn't be talking to me as he was about to do, and asked me not to tell anyone that he had done so. I was stunned at what he told me. First of all, Nanny was to be brought to the hospital to look after me, as we were going on a journey. He wouldn't say

23

where, but he insisted that we must have very warm clothes as it would be cold where we were going. He ran an unnecessary risk telling me all this. It was a humane kindness and, over the years, there were other Germans who were kind too – as well as those who were not.

Nanny was alerted and when she arrived to share the hospital room we speculated endlessly about our journey. Would it be Russia, or Siberia, or perhaps Germany, or even, wildest guess of all, might it be to go back home to England? So we waited, not knowing.

III
❦ The Camp ❧

FINALLY, ONE MORNING about 7 a.m. two German
Military policemen burst into the room with guns at the
ready, as though expecting Nanny and me to put up a
fight, or throw a bomb, or jump out of the window.
The nuns hovered anxiously, but were rudely shoved
back. The soldiers indicated that we must get dressed,
pack a suitcase and be ready to leave – NOW. They
refused to leave the room. Nanny asked if we could
bathe and dress in the little cubicle next door and, after
carefully inspecting it for possible escape holes, they
consented. One stayed in the room while the other
stood guard outside the tiny bathroom. That was to be
the last proper bath for the next four years.

With many shovings and proddings and cries of
Schnell and *Raus* – which was to become a familiar
chorus over the years – Nanny and I were pushed into
the back of a lorry. Many old friends were in it too,
having come from Châteauneuf. One family in particular we were pleased to be with: Mrs. Felix Dougall
and her three daughters. The eldest, Jean, was three
years older than me, and was a very pretty blond, and a
sweet girl. The other two, Clodagh and Maureen, were
nine and eleven. They also had their dog, a Schnautzer
named Bill, with them. Nothing would make them part
with him, and just because he was a German dog he was

allowed to accompany them. Felix Dougall was expecting another baby.

The first leg of the journey wasn't far. We were driven to the big barracks in Quimper, which was being used as a hospital and holding depot for French soldiers. As soon as we saw all the other English people there, we realized that this was the rounding-up point for the British in Brittany – mostly women, with a few children, but no boys over sixteen or men under sixty-five. The men had been taken to the vast, disused barracks in St. Denis, just outside Paris, where they spent the war. Jean's father and brother had gone there. I knew Peter well; we used to play table tennis together. Her father was crippled with polio, and could only just walk with a stick. Our one consolation was that we were all together.

At the barracks we were herded into one big room. It was full of double bunks and there must have been about forty of us British. A soldier was posted outside the door, armed of course, and if anyone wanted to go to the lavatory, he had to get another armed guard to accompany the prisoner and stand outside. French lavatories in barracks are extremely primitive – the familiar hole in the ground, with foot rests. It is very off-putting having an armed soldier waiting impatiently outside and occasionally shouting "*Schnell!*"

The French soldiers who were still in the barracks cooked for us.

That evening an English-speaking German officer burst into the room, clicked his heels formally and informed us we would be there for a few days: "You are not to move outside this room. Transport is being arranged for you all." Where to, was the burning question.

Jean and I were not particularly worried – no one was at that stage; the British are admirably phlegmatic in the

26

face of a crisis. We made ourselves as comfortable as possible, joked among ourselves and tried to amuse the young children. Jean and I would station ourselves at the windows and have flirtatious conversations with the French troops in other parts of the huge barracks, likewise at their windows and not allowed out. Sweets and notes were lowered on strings when the German sentries patrolling outside had passed, and a fairly light-hearted time was enjoyed by the two of us. Mrs. Dougall and Nanny did worry, though. A couple of days or so later the same German officer informed us we would leave by train the next morning: "Take some food with you. The journey may be long."

Nanny and Felix Dougall somehow organized, through the French staff, a couple of large tins of *"singe"* (the French nickname for bully beef, though the actual word means monkey!), a couple of large loaves of bread and a couple of bottles of water. This was a lifesaver – the water. We had formed ourselves into a group, the four Dougalls, their dog, Nanny and me.

On the morning of departure Nanny was, as usual, dealing out the so-called breakfast allotted to us – brown liquid, bearing no resemblance to coffee, and hunks of bread to dip in it. She was slicing the loaf, still in her dressing-gown, when the knife slipped and cut deeply into the vein in her wrist. She had been holding the loaf in her left hand and cutting towards her. Blood gushed from the wound. I made her lie down and hold the arm up, and then pounded on the door for the guard. He thought it was a trick until Nanny moved her other hand which she had clenched over the wound, and the blood streamed out. He made her lie on the concrete floor outside the room, with me beside her, while he got someone to fetch a doctor. It was a horrifying sight and I was in floods of tears, but Nanny was completely calm.

27

A French doctor arrived at last. He knew we were leaving, and goodness knows when she would get another dressing. Accompanied by the second guard he took her away to the surgery and stitched it up, bandaging it very carefully. Once again, one of the tiny miracles of the war was the fact that four days later, after the filth of the journey, there was no infection at all and it healed perfectly. Poor Nanny was shaken and very pale, but so brave. Jean and I carried her suitcase as well as Felix's and the children's.

Lorries took us to the station where we were prodded and pushed into a long train – wooden seats and four communicating compartments to each carriage. Two German guards were in each compartment, and had a whole side to themselves. The prisoners were crammed in like cattle, six a side with no sanitation and no water. More and more truckloads of British kept arriving and, despite the soldiers forbidding us to call to each other, we naturally did, cracking typically ridiculous British jokes: "Any more for the Skylark?"; "I wanted to go to Birmingham". . . . The Germans just couldn't understand our high spirits and lack of fear. If one was British one had no need to be be afraid, or so we thought. One was protected under the Geneva Convention.

At last the train could hold no more and began its snail-like journey. For the first few hours spirits were fairly high; it made a change from the barracks anyway. Bill was a great help – he was so good and Felix Dougall shared all her ration of food with him and wouldn't let anyone else give him anything.

The train wasn't heated at all and it was very cold. My thin school mac wasn't much protection. We were closely packed, but though the atmosphere was oppressive my feet were icy. Eventually calls of nature became urgent. What would be done about it? It couldn't have been simpler. The train just stopped in the middle of nowhere and we were shoved out and told to use the line. It must have been humiliating and embarrassing for some of the older people, but Jean and I, being used to a certain lack of privacy from schooldays, were not too upset by it. We sheltered each other.

We daren't eat too much of the bully beef and bread, as we had no idea how long the journey would take, or indeed where we were going. The first night was misery, trying to sleep bolt upright on seats that got harder and harder. Poor Nanny's wrist was throbbing and she obviously had a temperature. There was no question of washing, and we just had sips from the water bottle now and again. Occasionally the train would stop near a station – not near enough to see where it was – in order to round up more British subjects. The jolt of coaches being shunted on to the train was the only indication. The train got slower and slower, and by pressing our faces to the window when it was going round a bend we could see that it seemed to stretch for miles. By the second day everyone was stiff and sore and the water had run out. How we longed for a cup of tea! Bill whimpered gently, put his muzzle between his paws and went back to sleep. Eventually the train did stop near enough to a station for us to open the windows, hold out our empty bottles and plead for them to be filled. We were, in fact, *really* thirsty, a horrid feeling; food didn't seem to matter quite so much, even though we were extremely hungry too. The French people, who must have felt sorry for the train-load of misery, hastened to replenish our bottles and managed to throw some bread to us as well. They told us where we were – it was Rheims, only as far as Rheims after all that time! But spirits soared immediately. We were going steadily East; so more guessing started as to our destination. The third day the train was stopped for longer than usual and it was possible to have chats with those in neighbouring carriages, once we had relieved ourselves. The guards got a bit alarmed at this, and kept counting their respective charges in case one had escaped.

On the third night the train seemed to stop for good. It was in a siding and deep snow lay around. We were mauve with cold and could hardly move our lips. The two little girls, Clodagh and Maureen, held Bill on their laps to try to get some warmth. They were crying quietly with the cold and he licked their faces, trying to comfort them. The thoughts of cups of tea kept floating in our minds, and hot buttered toast and hot baths. Even a cup of the nasty brown "ersatz" coffee would have been more than welcome. Next morning we dis-embarked in the snow and were marched through the station to the waiting trucks. We saw that it was Besançon, high up in the mountains of the Haute-Saône. We could see, too, that there were literally thousands of us – and a very mixed bag, some babies, some very old, some hardly British at all. Because of being married to an Englishman or being born in a British colony, the poor things were lumped together as British. We shivered with cold and lack of food and sleep. How right the German Colonel had been when he warned us of a cold destination. Our hearts sank as we clambered into the open trucks waiting for us.

The trucks off-loaded us at the vast, disused, con-demned Besançon Barracks. A few Germans and a few French prisoners-of-war were wandering around, but they can't have known in advance what was coming or in what numbers. No preparations had been made at all. Various enormous blocks of buildings stood around a huge compound – bleak four-storey-high barracks. We shuffled our way up the echoing concrete steps of these freezing buildings. When we pushed open creaking door on the top floor words failed us. despair welled in our frozen bodies. The rooms were big – and utterly bare, not a bed or a chair or a table. Snow blew in through the broken window. The concrete floor was filthy. Forty people streamed into that room, and apart from our little group of eight, no one even spoke English! They were all French or Belgian or Polish.

We decided to occupy one half of a wall and to stay together at all costs. We longed for food; our last meal had been three days ago. The children were so hungry they had pains in their tummies and Mrs. Dougall was feeling pretty ill after such a journey. For the first time I realized how lucky I was to be responsible for no one and only have myself to worry about. Luckily, too, I had completely recovered from my operation.

Jean and I decided we must somehow organize beds for that very night. To lie on concrete in below-freezing temperatures might mean pneumonia. Down the stairs we clattered and into the great yard. The German guards were cold too, and had made a big bonfire. We warmed ourselves at it, and decided to chat up the soldiers and negotiate for beds. We didn't care what people thought if we were seen talking to Germans. Our German was pretty basic but we managed to put across the fact that the two little girls were exhausted and their mother was pregnant. I also explained about Nanny and her hand. An officer passed and I thought he must speak English if he was one of the officers in charge. He did, and we bombarded him with questions. We were told that a meal was being prepared for us by the French P.o.W.s, that there was a doctor, also a P.o.W., for Nanny and, best of all, he instructed the soldiers standing round the fire to rustle up as many beds as possible for our room. Jean and I bustled around. It was a relief to be moving and to get the circulation going. We found a store and were issued with straw mattresses – filthy, but blissful after the cold nights in the train. We explored further and found out where the kitchens, the hospital and the surgery were. Up and down those four flights of stone steps we went, glad to be useful, glad to be doing something which gave an illusion of warmth. We looked at each other and laughed! How could we have thought that we might get anywhere by flirting with German soldiers looking like we did? Our faces were streaked with dirt and our hair uncombed for days.

Standing in the middle of the floor of our room was an old-fashioned round, black stove. Somewhere there must be coal, but what were we to get it in? Once again we went on the scrounge, discovered an old tin, and once again asked anyone we saw who seemed to be in authority for coal. There was a ton of it in one of the sheds – our joy and pride was immense. How to light the fire though, with no wood and, ridiculous as it may sound, no paper either? Meanwhile the wooden bunks were slowly going up. They were double bunks, stacked painfully close together – and that was all the furniture there was to be for that day. Those who have seen Colditz on television will have got a very false idea of what a prison barrack-room looked like. The real ones were packed like sardines, and the bunks and mattresses were filthy with lice and bedbugs.

Nanny went to the French doctor who was amazed to see how clean her wound was; he put on another bandage. Jean and I fought our way to the kitchen with hundreds of others, and there we queued, a hundred yards or more, in the snow. People quarrelled, pushed and shoved and we had to exert all our strength to keep our place. We wondered, too, how we were going to carry any food. We had nothing to put it in, nor to eat it with! After an hour we reached the enormous urns where the "soup" was being ladled out. There were stacks of enamel bowls beside the soldiers dishing out the food. We explained we were fetching for eight, and were given eight spoons, eight knives and a washing-up-size bowl full of a watery soup, made from mangel-wurzels. We were also given a loaf of black German bread, more grey than black and hard as nails, and, incongruously enough, a plate with some dollops of a very solid red jam which tasted of nothing. However, we were literally starving by now and hurried back to our room, trying to keep the soup warm. The eight of us all ate out of it together and immediately felt much better. Nanny and Felix had got the big stove going, using some straw out of a mattress! What with the heat from that and forty bodies in a room meant for twenty soldiers, the place began to warm up.

There was a woman with a baby in the other half of the room, but there was no milk of course, and its pathetic cries got weaker and weaker. Our hearts bled for the mother, who was Belgian. She was beside herself with grief, screaming at the Germans and attacking the officer who came to our room to explain our position to us. The baby died two days later. That first night many of the old people died from the cold, particularly those who hadn't had young people in their rooms to ferret around for them. There were, on the whole, very few young.

The barracks had been built for around 2,000 soldiers and we were roughly 4,000 strong, so you can imagine how overcrowded it was. Out of that 4,000 probably only about 200 were English, as opposed to British.

BELLINGHAM HIGH SCHOOL LIBRARY 35842

The enamel bowl had to be used for everything – washing up, washing hair, washing clothes, washing ourselves! Having clattered downstairs for water, this was then heated on the stove in the same bowl. The main object that first afternoon was to acquire blankets, and again, by constant prowling around and peering and asking, Jean and I acquired enough for the group. It couldn't all be done in one journey obviously, and we must have been up and down those stairs fifty times on that first day. However, we did feel we had achieved wonders. In our searchings we had found cardboard for the broken window, and by nightfall it was practically home! The long queue for supper resulted in a jug of black ersatz coffee and a small piece of cheese to be eaten with any bread left over from lunch.

Nanny and Felix had rigged up a tiny washing corner – the enamel bowl on a box and a blanket draped round it for privacy. It meant more water-carrying, but we were determined to have a good wash despite the lack of soap.

The sanitary facilities were criminal. Long, open, outdoor lavatory blocks – about twenty or thirty in a row, behind each building. They were half-partitioned, and consisted of huge vats underneath a hole, with "rests" for feet. All this covered in ice – and so slippery that one or two people did actually slip into the filth below. These were emptied once in a blue moon by the French P.o.Ws. A nice touch was the fact that the lavatory block behind our building was looked after by a very old English jockey from Chantilly, and his name really was W. C. Bottom! He was endlessly cheerful, kept them as clean as he could and informed one which "throne" was empty.

Never had a bed seemed so comfy as the top bunk that night. We struggled into the straw, pulling the dark grey blankets up under our chins. The coughing and snoring, the crying of the baby, the weeping of its poor mother, the squabbling that went on all night, might have been miles away. We slept soundly until brutally awoken at 6 a.m. by a German sentry bursting into the room and telling us to *"Raus schnell"* down to the kitchen for breakfast. More black ersatz coffee (it tasted bitter and awful, but it was hot), and more German loaves: that was all. Again we queued, in the dark, in the snow, for our rations for eight. By the time we got back the others were up and the fire was alight. Nanny had slept in the bottom bunk and Jean in the top bunk of the one alongside, so close one could reach over and touch the next one. The two little girls shared a bottom one, and Mrs. Dougall had one of the few single wooden beds, which she shared with Bill. This was in the corner, and had a little privacy, except from the people directly opposite.

That morning one of the English-speaking German officers came to each room, making a complete list of names for a daily roll call, and to tell us of various distribution points for extra clothing, utensils, etc. He also asked for a number of volunteers to go out for two hours each morning to peel the mangel-wurzels that a French soldier had to split with a heavy axe. They were huge. He would point at certain people at random, saying: "You, you, you and you." Obviously Nanny, with her bad hand, and Mrs. Dougall couldn't stand in the snow for two hours, nor the little girls, so while they saw to "making the beds" and tidying the room, Jean and I undertook this chore willingly. It was quite fun – teasing the poor French soldier over his aim with the axe, chatting to inmates from other buildings, speculating again about how long it would all last, and doing as little as possible! An officious German sentry would prod the odd slacker with his gun, and Jean and I would poke our tongues out at him behind his back and feel very daring.

The issue of extra clothing was very welcome. It consisted of surplus 1914–1918 French soldiers' uniforms. This was useless for most of the women, who were too small, but I was delighted. I managed to find a pair of breeches that fitted, with puttees to wind round my legs to keep warm (up till then I had been wearing a skirt and school socks!), a pair of army boots that fitted and, my pride and joy, a double-breasted greatcoat. It nearly reached down to my ankles and was in good condition. I thought I looked terrific! Even Jean was quite complimentary, though rather envious, as she was tiny and nothing would fit her. We trotted on down to the big entrance gates – now closed and barred, with two sentries on duty – where there was a full-length mirror, used, in the days of the barracks' functional life, to see that the French soldiers were properly dressed before going into Besançon. It was the only mirror in the camp.

The Camp Commandant was a reasonable man. Mrs. Dougall and Nanny went to see him to ask about letters, about extra rations for the children, and about contacting the International Red Cross. Letters were out of the question; there were not enough staff for censoring. The rations were looked into and after a few weeks there was some milk for the girls and some extra food, like biscuits. After all, what we were then getting was inadequate for anyone, let alone a growing child.

The barrack square was huge and, despite the cold and the snow, day after day the camp inmates would trudge round it for exercise, and to get out of the overcrowded and extremely smelly rooms.

After a few days, to make it easier for the kitchens, the loaves of black German bread were issued from one central point by the simple method of throwing the loaves that each group of eight was allowed per week into a blanket held ready. The loaves were always mouldy and hard.

There was little time to think, with so many chores to do each day, but I vaguely imagined that everyone caught up in the war must be undergoing the same sort of existence. At the same time, half of me realized that mine was a unique case, since I had no parents with me. There seemed to be few other young in the camp and Jean and her sisters at least had their mother with them.

One or two incidents I remember vividly. There were, among the 4,000 or so inmates, many nuns from various Convents and Religious orders throughout France. Some of them had held the vow of silence for twenty years or more. For them prison life seemed an enchanting freedom. The Germans respected them and they were allowed to be together in their rooms, not all mixed up as we were. They were also allowed to wear their habits. Occasionally, on the very icy patches, a nun would be seen skating along, with her coiffe and habit billowing, shrieking with delight! Their rooms were spotless and not overcrowded, and for some inexplicable reason they got extra rations.

As you can imagine, among so many people from such widely different backgrounds, there were some very talented ones. There were actresses, musicians, artists and singers. Though there were less than three weeks to go to Christmas, they were determined to put on a variety show for the camp. Where to hold it? There was only one hut not in use, and it would only hold about three or four hundred. It had to be there. Jean and I never thought we would get in, but by that date so many people were ill, or too old to want to go out in the icy dark, that only 2,000 or so battled for the precious

37

seats. No one checked the numbers, but nearly 1,000 must have crowded in. The Germans had been asked if the French and English National Anthems could be sung at the end of the concert, and this had been refused. The Germans also insisted on having the front two rows!

Jean and I were near the back, but we could see and hear well. It was a stunning show. Somehow scenery and curtains had been made – costumes and make-up conjured up out of thin air; even a piano had been unearthed. There were hilarious sketches, mercilessly poking fun at the Germans – too subtle for the Germans to understand, but which the audience loved. We were doubled up with laughter and the applause for every act was thunderous. The song "*J'attendrai*" had been given new words about escaping prisoners, brilliantly done, and so simple that the audience sang the chorus lustily. "The Lambeth Walk" was given the same treatment and, when it came to the lines "Why don't you go there – stay there", the performers all pointed at the Germans with complete disregard for possible retribution.

Everyone forgot their discomfort, their cold and hunger, their loneliness and their imprisonment. We wished the evening could go on forever. The encores and cheers reached fever pitch. Near the end, in a marked pause and in complete silence, the Germans solemnly filed out. This was the Camp Commandant's unacknowledged admission that nothing could stop the whole hut singing the National Anthems. It was tactful of him and it was widely appreciated. They sang the *Marseillaise* first; after all there were far more French there than English. The entire cast filled the stage and led the singing, with the piano for accompaniment. The audience stood on chairs, on each other's shoulders, packed like sardines. The rendering of "God save the

King" must have been heard in Besançon. Never has it been sung with so much emotion, so much loyalty and pride. How it was even sung is a miracle, as tears were streaming from everyone's eyes. It was a unique occasion; everyone there knew that they would remember that evening all their lives, and that, whenever the anthems were played, that particular occasion would immediately be conjured up in their minds. It wasn't until the end of the war that I next heard the National Anthem played and I couldn't refrain from crying at the memory of that night in Besançon camp. I sometimes wonder how many are still alive today who were there, and in what corners of the world they are now scattered.

Possibly because of my height, and perhaps also because I was completely bilingual, I was made a policewoman, with an armband on my greatcoat. This meant that when the canteen was opened for an afternoon, perhaps twice a week, I was one of the people who had to try and control the queue. It should be remembered that there were some very tough types there – and tough women are harder to deal with than any man. The canteen sold cigarettes, a few oranges, a strange grey gritty substance that was supposed to be soap, and occasionally bottles of beer. I never went in. I was too busy outside in the snow trying to stop the women fighting. They would pull each other's coats off in their frenzy to achieve one or two extras. The other reason why I never went in was that I had no money. It made life much simpler. My other job was taking the roll call on a particular floor in a different building to ours. This had to be done early on in the evening, when everyone had to be in their rooms for the night. The reason for it being in a strange block was that I wouldn't be tempted to let a name I knew go by without a response. It was an unpleasant job. I was only fifteen and some of the hardened cases gave me a rough time. It was while doing this job that I found out how pleasant, quiet and clean the nuns' rooms were.

Quite soon after we got to Besançon, Nanny discovered that people in our room had lice in their hair, so she cut mine off, short as a boy's, so that it could easily be washed in that same old bowl! There were bed bugs too. They bit, and smelt horrid when they were squashed. Nanny got some disinfectant from the hospital and poured it over the beds. It got rid of them for a bit, but eventually the rooms had to be fumigated.

A number of people, due to the constant diet of mangel-wurzels, got gastro-enteritis, an agonizing complaint, especially in the bitter cold nights, when four flights of stone steps had to be negotiated in the dark, plus a hundred yards or so, in the snow and icy winds, to the latrines. I got it too, and often thought I would never make it to the latrines in time. I have never got rid of it completely; all through my life it has recurred. There was no medicine and no treatment. There were too many old people, desperately ill, needing the few hospital beds and the meagre supply of drugs.

Suddenly one day, quite unexpectedly, a Red Cross truck arrived. The driver and his two helpers were besieged by people wanting news of relatives or hoping to get out of the camp, but most of all anxious to find out how the war was going. That was the most frustrating part of it – having no news, no papers, no letters, no wireless.

After a couple of months, our little group of eight managed to move into a small room with just six double bunks and two beds. This seemed sheer luxury. It also had a window one could look out of. The one on our side of the old room had been too small and too high up to see out of. I made some sketches of the camp and the rooms, but unfortunately they were confiscated. We acquired a table and two benches and felt quite civilized. Somehow Nanny produced a broom and some more utensils, and kept the room spotless.

The camp became slightly less congested as slowly, day by day, people were released, either on account of ill health or their age. The Red Cross, after their visit, must have told the Germans that they had no right to detain the over-sixties or indeed the under-sixteens.

About this time, in February, 1941, many educational courses were started up in the camp. Numerous professors of every subject one could think of organized these. One could study maths, theology, chess, philosophy, art, anything. Nanny gently hinted that I might like to take advantage of this schooling, but I refused! Like any self-respecting schoolgirl, I didn't see why I should: it was the one recompense for being in a camp. I also argued that I was much too busy carting water and coal, peeling the endless mangel-wurzels, queuing for meals, etc. Nanny didn't have the heart to insist!

If there was ever a bit of potato or meat in our big bowl of soup, Nanny would make sure I got my share, and Felix Dougall did the same for Clodagh and Maureen. We all gave a bit to Bill. How he survived on that total lack of meat no one could understand. Now and again the German officer would come into the room and shout hysterically and say Bill would have to go; but Clodagh and Maureen, who were fair, with big brown eyes, would sob their eyes out and, as the weeks went by, we realized that the threat was meaningless.

One day the camp was informed over the loudspeakers that enough Red Cross parcels had arrived for everyone and could be collected straight away. The excitement was tremendous; it was like a delayed

Christmas. Everyone rushed back to their rooms to gloat over the contents of their parcels. It was a real thrill to see things like tea and cocoa and soap that would lather. But alas, one tragedy soon became apparent. The delicious-looking chocolate all tasted of soap! In fact, anything that wasn't in a tin tasted of soap. The disappointment was bitter. So lovingly packed, so thoughtfully and carefully assembled – all ruined. There was no way of using the tea or cocoa as we didn't have access to any hot water. We mixed it in with the ersatz coffee, but it has to be admitted that it didn't improve the flavour! Still, the cocoa tasted quite nice mixed in with the sticky red jam we had on alternate days for supper. There were tins of sardines and spam too, and thereafter the parcels started to come regularly every few weeks.

It was at about this time that my knowledge of sex increased. When I was taking the nightly roll-call I noticed, in one of the big rooms, two women in one bed. I told Nanny about it and asked her if she could do something about block B, as in one of the rooms there were not enough beds and women were having to share. Darling Nanny, a spinster, but full of understanding, sympathy and love for everyone, then had to explain about lesbianism to a bewildered fifteen-year-old. I thought about it, and it dawned on me that that was what the girls at my boarding school were. Again I asked Nanny and she explained that it was quite different at that age. Jean and I had great giggles about it, in the cruel way of the young, and speculated about various women from then on.

Suddenly in March it got hotter. The snow seemed to melt overnight and the sun shone. Then the realization that we couldn't go anywhere to enjoy it hit us, and apathy, boredom and disease hit the camp. Jean and I would sunbathe in the afternoon in our two-hour "free" period, and talk of food and men, and food and love, and food and escaping. We were both very thin; the diet of watery soup and mouldy bread had taken its toll after nearly four months.

One afternoon Mrs. Dougall and I heard our names called over the loudspeaker, telling us to report to the Camp Commandant. We both wondered what it could mean and turned up at his office feeling sick with apprehension. He told us that we were to be released in a few days' time, Mrs. Dougall because of the two girls and I because of my age. He wanted to know if there was anyone who could provide accommodation for us. We obviously couldn't go back to Brittany. Just think what a threat a pregnant woman, a Schnautzer, two little girls and a teenager would present to the Germans if they were allowed to live near the coast! Mrs. Dougall had friends in Paris and the Commandant arranged for them to be contacted. My only contact in France was my cousin in Brittany. Her in-laws, the Provosts, lived in Paris and it was decided that they could arrange somewhere for me to live.

Excited though I was, I hated the thought of leaving Nanny and Jean behind. I was also apprehensive about being on my own in Paris.

A week or so elapsed before the Commandant summoned us once more and gave us the addresses we were to go to.

Four months had passed since the day we had driven into Besançon barracks and when twenty or so of us marched out on that sunny day at the end of March, it was an incredible feeling. We waved to our friends and Felix and I had lumps in our throats, while Bill barked furiously. He couldn't understand why the whole family wasn't going out together on this first proper walk. Jean was in tears; luckily she was released later when her mother had the baby, as there was no one to look after them. Amazingly enough, the baby, another daughter, was strong and healthy, despite the lack of nutrition during the first months of pregnancy. She later became a brilliant scholar and went to university.

Before we left the camp we were searched and our passports were given back to us. It was during this search that my sketches and a diary I had been writing were confiscated.

Nanny was to remain an internee for the whole war, but later that year the whole camp was transferred to Vittel, in Vichy France, where hotels had been requisitioned, and where they were much more comfortable. However, I didn't find out about this move until after the war, as there were no letters and it distressed me continually to think of Nanny still at Besançon. She became a "chef de secteur" (head of a large part of one of the hotels) and also helped to organize some successful escapes.

IV
❦ Paris ❧

MY COUSIN DIANA arranged for me to stay in a little
guest house in Neuilly, a very pleasant district of Paris.
It was a most attractive house in the leafy Boulevard
Jean Mermoz. It was very quiet and had a garden, and
my little room had a balcony. To me it was as though I
had walked straight into Heaven. Three dear spinster
sisters ran it, Mesdemoiselles Thérèse, Gabrielle and
Marie. They were kind but strict. I remember little of
the train journey to Paris or the taxi to Neuilly; it all
seemed like a dream. The fact that I had a room of my
own, with a proper lavatory nearby and a basin actually
in my room, though only with cold water – there was
no fuel for hot water, was unbelievably wonderful.

Slowly I regained my health. I suffered from boils and
carbuncles as a result of the bad food in the camp, and
was strangely tired, which is unnatural at that age, but
was probably another legacy of Besançon.

The restrictions on my freedom were not too oner-
ous. I had to sign every day at the Commissariat of
Police, which was nearby so not too irksome, and I had
to be in by nightfall – no problem in summer, and
winter was still a long way off. Needless to say I was not
allowed outside Paris, but that was not really a restric-
tion.

The other guests at the *pension* were a mixed bunch.
They seemed terribly old to me, but must have been no

45

more than middle-aged. There was a Professor who ate noisily. He did not like the British and would pick his teeth and shake his head sadly at me and say "Ah! If the English had not left us in the lurch, you wouldn't be here on your own now." I had to repeat my eternal refrain endlessly: "I got left behind by mistake. My mother thought she could come back for me, but in Brittany we didn't know how near the Germans were. But *we* are still fighting and we will *win*." I didn't feel all that confident then, but could not bear to have my country criticized.

Throughout the entire war I had no news whatsoever of my parents, nor, indeed, did they know what was happening to me, which was probably fortunate in view of what was to come. In fact, at this time my father was regrouping to form the 6th Armoured Division. The only news in the French newspapers was of the sinking of British ships, great "German Victories", according to the French newspapers.

Another guest was a businessman who tucked his table-napkin under his chin and greedily wiped his plate with his bread. He was an even noisier eater than the professor, and tried to be jolly. Two spinsters, rather genteel and disapproving of nearly everything, and a young girl in her twenties, made up the numbers. The young girl seemed old to me too! She was studying and was very kind to me, but obviously terrified of actually speaking to, and living under the same roof as, an English girl.

As in England at that time, food was severely rationed. Even potatoes were rationed, as well as the usual items, such as bread, sugar, meat and butter. The "Demoiselles" were very fair and made the best of the available food. Wine was also rationed which seems funny, but as it is such a staple part of the French diet it was counted as food. We were allowed two litres per person per week; as I didn't drink wine the other guests in the pension were extra-nice to me in order to have my share! The other unusual rationed item was a quarter of a bottle of brandy a month per person. This I kept. There being nothing to put the sugar in, I used to dip my two lumps a day in the brandy and have them as a treat in the evening.

Diana Provost's mother-in-law lived in Paris and sometimes she asked me to lunch at weekends. The meals were fantastic, with no sign of rationing and lamb and butter from Brittany. Madame Provost (senior) was a firm *"Pétainiste"* (which meant she supported the Vichy Government), so, tactfully, I didn't talk about the war. It was kind of her to ask me to lunch, especially at weekends, when I was lonely and hungry. There was also another family who were very kind and hospitable to me. They used to stay in Concarneau in the summer, which was how I came to know them. Their daughter, Sylvie Feuillatte, was a great friend of mine. The Feuillate family were also staunch *"Pétainistes"* at that stage of the war.

All through the war, even though I didn't see my cousin till near the end of it, she made herself financially responsible for me. She paid the *pension* and the school, which was incredibly kind of her, as no one knew when the two families might be reunited to sort out their affairs. Diana let me have her bicycle too, which was essential for school, and fun to cycle round Paris on. Except for German tanks and cars and public transport, there was no other traffic, which made it safe and easy for the cyclist, so I got to know Paris quite well. One day in April, 1941, about a month after I had settled in, Sylvie and I rode to the Champs Elysées and sat at a café. We watched silently, sick at heart, as German soldiers marched in an endless goose-step up the Avenue. They sang, too: "*Wir fahren gegen Engelland*" . . . "We are marching on England". They sang so harmoniously; it was an unforgettable, horrific sight which I took care never to witness again.

April in Paris has been so often described. The chestnut trees, both pink and white, were flowering all along the Boulevard Jean Mermoz, and somehow the beauty of the city rose above the shame and horror of the occupation. It hurt dreadfully, of course, to see the swastika flying from the top of the Eiffel Tower, under the Arc de Triomphe, and outside the doors of the luxury hotels in the Rue de Rivoli and Rue St. Honoré. The cafés and shops were full of Germans, all still behaving very correctly and politely, but completely ostracized. It was a loathsome sight to see them saluting each other with the Heil Hitler salute in the bar of the George V Hotel in the Champs Elysées.

Bicycling around, I got to know parts of Paris quite well. Sylvie and I and her young brother Nicholas explored together. We didn't talk about the war or politics or religion. At that age one could ignore the "*boches*", "*les haricots verts*" as they were called ("green beans", because of the colour of their uniforms, which were greeny grey).

Sylvie was eighteen and had left school, while I resigned myself to going back to school once more, but as a day girl now. That was much nicer than being a boarder, with the thought of the comfy little room in the *pension* as my sanctuary.

My school in the Cours Montaigne was near enough for me to bicycle back to lunch each day. The girls there were helpful and friendly, and I was put in a form of girls about a year younger than me. I was surprised to see that English was allowed to be taught, but refused to take those lessons! The maths teacher was a very brilliant woman, both understanding and charming, and for the first time ever, I grasped the nettle of maths and actually started getting problems right. I talked and thought in French; I even dreamt in French!

Living in such a lovely and remote part of Paris, it was easy to ignore the nastier aspects of the Germans, such as the spot checks that went on at the Metro entrances to find out if people's papers were in order. One heard rumours of arrests for sabotage, and heard stories about the persecution of the Jews. But all these things happened so gradually to begin with that one was hardly aware of them.

The summer was long and hot. Our small group of friends would bicycle to a club in the Bois de Boulogne to swim. It was the year of "surprise parties" (the French borrowed our word "surprise" and gave it a French pronunciation), and occasionally I would be invited. I was conscious of the fact that I only had two dresses, but no one cared about clothes. Sometimes it was worrying if I was late returning to the *pension*. There was always the risk of a randon check by the Germans and the three spinsters were responsible for me. They took it in turn to give me firm but gentle advice. Once or twice I stayed with Sylvie's relations outside Paris over a weekend. This involved clever signing at the Commissariat – one large signature covering two days before going away and the same on one's return, hoping they hadn't noticed one's absence!

Funnily enough, another activity that was strictly forbidden was fishing! This was a big joke among my teenage friends: "Are you taking the boat out today? Make sure you catch enough fish to keep you going till you reach England!" Not particularly funny, but at the time it had many variations and was hilarious.

The spinsters were terrified of my being caught trying to listen to the B.B.C. on their wireless. It was daring enough to harbour an English girl, albeit legitimately, right under the Germans' noses. Nevertheless, occasional snippets of news were gleaned – the landings in North Africa, Churchill's speeches, and the baffling sentences which were coded messages to the Resistance and the British Intelligence operators dropped by parachute into France. They held an awesome fascination for me, and I longed to know what they meant, wishing I were old enough to do something useful, instead of just boring old school.

Jean Dougall's brother Peter was in the barracks of St. Denis, as I mentioned earlier. Once a month I was allowed to visit him. This was a great adventure. I would take a huge parcel of whatever food I could wangle, and a litre of my ration of wine. The barracks was a bleak, depressing place, and the large hut where the visiting took place was unromantic. There were wide trestle tables going round the hut, and the prisoners were on the inside, while the visitors stayed on the outside. German guards patrolled constantly and we weren't supposed to touch each other. Peter and I were about the same age, fifteen and sixteen, and very shy. After a few months, Peter waited for the guard's back to be turned and stretched out his arm across the wide table; I did the same, and for a few seconds we held hands. He was deeply moved and I felt desperately sorry for him. With all chance of a serious education gone, what would become of him? When I left he leant across and kissed me on the cheek, and I hadn't the heart to tell him I didn't feel the same way. I felt so guilty at being free while he was in prison. As the months passed, he fell in love with me and made me a ring out of a two-franc piece – with "*liberté, égalité, fraternité* on it – and asked me to marry him. I knew how much it would help him through the long years of internment, so I accepted. I thought that somehow events would sort it all out for me, and it was an easy pretence to keep up – a chaste kiss on the mouth when I arrived for the hour-long visit which, after all, only took place once a month. He became ambitious for our future and took advantage of the various courses open to him in the prison camp, thus shaking off the fatal boredom of prisoners. I felt that his attitude was so important that it didn't matter that I was playing a false role. Nevertheless the visits were a great ordeal for me, as the duplicity seemed so wrong and it upset me. It was difficult to talk freely at St. Denis, with so many people elbowing their way on to the bench that faced inwards. Peter felt it was a disgrace that he would perhaps miss out on the war altogether. Sometimes he would hardly talk at all and just stare moodily and enviously at me, with the same deep brown eyes of his sisters. He wanted to escape but I knew it would be impossible for him. His French was poor, he had no money, and his chances of reaching England nil. If he were caught, he would either be sent to Germany, or, as he was sixteen and not in uniform, might well be shot. I persuaded him to stay with his father, who was so badly crippled with polio he could barely walk. As the summer turned to autumn and the term began, it became more difficult to get to see him. The journey took over an hour, and food was becoming more and more difficult to get hold of.

The last time I saw him was at his confirmation in the Cathedral of St. Denis, a truly magnificent building. There was an ordination of Roman Catholic priests, and a priest internee, by sheer persuasion and persistence, managed to get permission for the few internee confirmation candidates to be included in this ceremony. I still have the invitation to it in my Bible. It was a unique service. The glory and panoply of the French Roman Catholic ordination, with the novitiate priests prostrating themselves in their beautiful copes, the handful of thin, tidily, but poorly dressed young prisoners, and, of course, the most stark and horrific contrast of all – the hundred or more German armed guards lolling against the soaring pillars, guns at the ready. It was a truly noble gesture of the Roman Catholics thus to allow the sacrilege of their Cathedral. I was not the only one in tears.

At about this time Mrs. Dougall had her baby and Jean was released to look after her mother and the girls. It was wonderful to meet up with her again and to have news of Nanny. We couldn't meet often because of school. I *had* to work hard at all the subjects and would study and read late into the night. The days grew shorter and colder. It was dark by the time I bicycled back from school, so it was lucky that Neuilly was a quiet district with very few Germans about. I realized that until March or April I would not be able to go out at all after school because of the curfew imposed on the few British who were still at liberty.

There was no heating or hot water anywhere in Paris, and the pension was no exception, but Mademoiselle Gabrielle, who was my favourite of the three sisters, used to fill a hot water bottle for me to go to bed with, and I would wash in that water in the morning, shivering in the cold. The balcony had lost its charm and the French windows leading on to it let in a lot of cold air. I had to keep reminding myself how lucky I was not to be still in the camp! It snowed and bicycling and walking without proper boots became a wet and slushy business. The meals were too meagre to warm one, breakfast consisting of one slice of bread with jam – no butter and no milk – and the by-now famous "berry coffee". Lunch was a miracle of house-keeping by the Demoiselles Dupont, with rabbit stew or horse meat (which the French eat anyway and which is very good – stronger flavoured than beef and disease free), or offal and a few vegetables, nearly always followed by some cheese and fruit. No tea, because the French don't have it, but some noodles or soup or occasionally eggs for supper. I was always hungry, but so was everyone else. I wondered endlessly about my parents. Over a year had passed since I had said goodbye to my mother in June, 1940. If only I could let her know that I was safe and well looked after. Later on I was glad that my mother did *not* know what was happening to me. Diana wrote to me often from Brittany which now seemed very far away and remote.

I had not had a strict religious upbringing, but now I felt that I wanted to go to Church. There being no Church of England Church to go to, I decided to contact the local French Protestant Minister. In my ignorance I imagined the French Protestant religion would be much the same as our Church of England. My faith was simple and straightforward; I believed all the teachings of the Bible implicitly and unquestioningly. Never had religion been discussed or doctrine queried. I arranged with the Vicar, or Pasteur, to attend confirmation classes as I was now sixteen. The minister was an elderly man and the classes were held in his house, with six other candidates, all French. The teachings seemed strange to me from the start, but I didn't really know what to expect, and it wasn't until the third lesson that I realized with sickening horror that they did not believe in the Virgin Birth or the Immaculate Conception. I cannot describe what a shattering revelation this was. Never had it dawned on me that such beliefs even existed; to hear them talked about quite casually seemed so blasphemous that I felt physically sick. Blushing crimson, I got to my feet, an anguished and embarrassed sixteen-year-old, and, interrupting the minister, I blurted out, "We don't believe the same things – your religion is wrong." Then I fled from his house, never to return.

Nowadays, with books like *Honest to God* written by actual men of the Church, all teenagers are used to having strange and unnatural ideas discussed all round them. But in 1941 it was a different matter, and I was shaken to the core. I didn't know what to do or who to talk to and felt guiltily foolish. It remained a secret and traumatic thought and for a long time the scar remained. In a way I felt tainted, and though strongly moved to become a Roman Catholic, I was too shy and inefficient to attempt any definite action. That was the end of my religious education until after the war, though my beliefs went full circle during the next couple of years.

The penetrating cold of that January of 1942 and a flu virus which claimed me as a victim resulted in pneumonia. It suddenly hit me as I was riding my bicycle through the slush. I fell off and, coughing and wheezing, painfully made my way back to the *pension*. There was no penicillin in 1942, so pneumonia was quite serious. The spinsters were very worried and found some wood for the little stove in my room. The blissful warmth vied with my soaring temperature and made me forget the bitter cold winter. I lost count of time, lying there sweating and delirious. Eventually a nurse was found, as I was too weak to get up. It was a bad patch; the gastro-enteritis struck again and I had one boil after another, always on my face! The pain from them was excruciating. The only treatment was hot fomentations until the boil burst and then to keep it as clean as possible. I felt so weak and longed for Nanny to come and look after me. I cried a lot, selfishly thinking only of myself and how ill I felt. My hair fell out in handfuls and great bald patches appeared, which terrified me. Sylvie told me to massage my scalp night and morning with my fingertips, and when, after a few weeks, I felt better, this treatment, unbelievably, worked. In the meantime I wore a black velvet snood to cover the baldness! I missed about a month of the spring term.

The behaviour of the Germans worsened in the spring in 1942, as was demonstrated by their treatment of the Jews, who were now obliged to wear a big yellow star on their sleeve. All cafés, cinemas and shops in Paris were full of German officers and soldiers, and all these public places were forbidden to the Jews, who could not even use public transport. Every now and again there would be a spot check, ostensibly to look at identity cards, but in reality as an excuse to bundle any Jews caught in the trap into a truck and away. At the beginning it was believed they were sent to prison or internment camps like Besançon, but soon the rumours got around of concentration camps and forced labour under appalling conditions. Though the extermination camps were still not public knowledge, people near station yards became aware, with horror, that the trucks these poor wretched Jews were herded into like cattle had a thick coating of lime on the floor. This ensured that, as it got wet on the journey, the fumes killed off many before they reached their journey's end. As yet, however, it was a whispered rumour, that no one could quite assimilate. How could one believe that the same Germans, officers and soldiers alike, who crowded into the opera, the concerts, the ballet and the Palais de Chaillot were capable of such behaviour?

In any case, that summer was an extremely anxious time for me, which left me little time to think of such matters. I was going to sit the pré-Baccalauréat – the French equivalent of 'O' levels. The work for me was doubly hard, especially the grammar, and I was eternally grateful for the two years I had spent in Concarneau, learning grammar every day until it became part of me. The French standard of education was much higher then, as indeed it is now, than the English.

The Baccalauréat differs from 'O' levels and 'A' levels in that there is a written *and* an oral examination on every single subject. I read and revised every night until my eyes closed. After all, I would be the only English girl among the thousands of examinees and I mustn't let the side down. There was a nagging worry, too, in that I had had my sixteenth birthday the previous September. Sooner or later I might be arrested again. In a way I would have been delighted to rejoin Nanny, but hoped it would not be before the exams.

These took place at the Sorbonne on the Left Bank. Day after day I went there by Metro in a sort of trance, lost in the vastness of it all. It was a stiflingly hot summer but the huge silent examination hall was cooler than outside. I wrote endlessly and, it seemed, curiously effortlessly, as in a dream. I could hardly believe it, but the very bits I had revised in history, French literature and other subjects seemed to be the main questions in all the papers. I knew the maths would be difficult, but managed to tackle the algebra and geometry. The written part was straight-forward, seated at a desk, with everyone concentrating on their own papers. The two days of the orals were a tremendous strain. These took place in a sort of indoor arena; the professors were at separate tables in the circle in the centre, and all around them rose tier upon tier of benches. The names of the examinees were called out loud, and they went from one master's table to another, being questioned. My heart missed several beats when my name was called. "Lyon-Smith" in French sounds very Jewish, especially the "Schmidt" part, and all heads turned to stare at me as I walked down the rows of seats to the awe-inspiring circle. My confidence was helped when the first examiner asked me to talk of two works from my favourite poets, Villon and Verlaine. Once again my luck held, except in English, when I was asked to talk about wheat-growing in Canada! Stupidly I had never attended the English classes at the Cours Montaigne, thinking I didn't need to. I hadn't spoken English for over a year and was terribly aware of how much I had forgotten. I was ashamed. Not only did I know nothing of crops in Canada, but I was unable to answer a single question on English grammar, a subject hardly touched on in English schools. Needless to say it was the one subject of the pré-Baccalauréat I failed to pass. The oral maths was a bit daunting. I was given a piece of chalk and a geometry problem to solve on a huge blackboard, explaining out loud as I went along. It was to do with tangents and circles and I literally fluffed my way through it, helped enormously by a white-haired professor with a great sense of humour. By this time it was realized that I was English and a certain sympathy must have swayed the final results!

Weeks later I received my certificate. Miracle of miracles, I had passed, though admittedly only with the "*mention*" or grade "*assez bien*". Somehow I managed to keep that small certificate, safely rolled up, through all my subsequent vicissitudes, and it is still one of my most treasured possessions.

Meanwhile in Brittany my cousin Diana was getting more and more worried about my safety. She had a great friend who knew how to get hold of false identity papers. This friend, Titi de Penarose, also knew of a farm near Bordeaux where the farmer, for a considerable fee, would let people cross over his land into unoccupied France. This area of unoccupied France was ruled by the Vichy Government. Diana and Titi organized this between them and when all was more or less settled Titi told me of the projected plan. The vital, all important part was total secrecy. No one, but no one, was to know I was leaving Paris.

I longed to tell Jean or Sylvie, yet I knew I mustn't. It seemed incredibly difficult to go bicycling together, to visit the baby sister, Joanna, and Mrs. Dougall, and make plans for a picnic a week or ten days hence, and know I wouldn't be there. All woman find secrets hard to keep (obviously I'm not talking about trained intelligence or resistance workers), but for me, the foolish girl who lived from day to day in a selfish world, soon to be so rudely shattered, it seemed an impossibility. I hated not telling the kind Demoiselles Dupont who had been home and parents to me for over a year. Obviously my disappearance would have to be explained somehow, so it was agreed that I would write an impassioned love-sick note and leave it in my little room, saying I had eloped with a boyfriend. It seemed a criminal thing to do to them. They would be so upset, having been strict but kind to me and I had never lied to them or stayed out late without telling them, or misbehaved in any way. At least it would absolve them from any blame when they were questioned by the police and then the Germans, as they were bound to be. Their genuine and total ignorance could not be feigned.

I would not be able to take much with me. I smuggled

out a few clothes and a few books each time I went out on my bicycle, and took them to Titi's flat. Titi gave me my false identity card. My new name was Marie Cornet. I needed it in advance in order to book a seat on a train to Bordeaux. Because Bordeaux was so near the unoccupied zone, and because so many people were trying to escape into unoccupied France by now, this irksome regulation had been introduced. One queued at a counter, producing one's identity card, stating where one was going, and why; and then waited for ages until one's name was called before getting the actual ticket and paying for it.

I was scared stiff. I felt so guilty when I produced my false *carte d'identité*. I was convinced it must be obvious it was a fake – but no, it passed off smoothly. The man behind the counter asked exactly where I was going, and why, and I gave the name of a village close to Bordeaux, saying I went to visit my aunt there every summer. I looked too young, with no make-up and straight hair, to be suspected of anything, and I was asked to wait until they checked when the next train to Bordeaux with a spare seat would be running. They had to call my name several times before I realized "Mademoiselle Marie Cornet" meant *me*! I was sure this would give the game away, but, with so much hustle and bustle going on, it wasn't noticed.

Among the few personal possessions I took with me was my Teddy Bear. I'd had him as a child, never having liked dolls, and I was very attached to the bald and ageing bear. He went everywhere with me.

Soon there were only two days to go. I was so excited that it was practically impossible to hide it. One of the nicest things was the thought of no more school! Also I was going to meet a very sweet person called Ruth Peters. She was Diana's cousin, but not in fact related to me. She was Canadian, but had lived in France a long time, and had spent the war in a little village near Grenoble. Titi had told me that, once I was over the frontier, I should catch a train to another small station, not too far away, so as not to arouse suspicion, and from there take a train to Grenoble where Ruth Peters would meet me. All these preparations had been carefully thought out for me. After all, I had never travelled in a train, or any other form of public transport, on my own!

On my last day in Paris I signed my name in the book in the police station for three days. With luck they wouldn't notice I hadn't been in for two days, and by then I would be safely over the border into so-called Free France with no more Germans around. I couldn't wait. It had been hateful and galling to witness their arrogance and pride in Paris. Every day their crack troops, complete with band and singing lustily, would goose-step up the Champs Elysées. After a few months of this all the French people went indoors, so as not to give them the satisfaction of an audience. I had lived far enough away not to see this performance often, but the sight of their hated uniforms with "*Got mitt uns*" on their belts, their endless "*Heil Hitlers*" and the hundreds of loathsome fluttering swastika flags, made me seethe with anger and hatred. Their brutal, callous and needlessly cruel reprisals towards the French civilian population were by now widely known and dreaded. I was leaving all this for ever, and might even reach England via Spain or Switzerland, from the free zone. The thought of seeing my parents again was an immense joy.

V

☙ A Brush with Death ☙

NEEDLESS TO SAY I hardly slept at all that last night in my little room. My heart beat fast and many emotions filled me: fear – of the unknown, excitement – at the adventure, and some sadness at leaving the familiar and happy surroundings at the *pension*. I wrote the letter to a fictitious boy friend, and pinned it to the pillow in the conventional manner. I just couldn't swallow my *"tartine"* (slice of bread) and café at breakfast, causing Mademoiselle Gabrielle to fuss: "But you must be ill, *ma petite*, have you got a temperature?" Unable to speak properly, with tears not far off, I reassured her and said I was going off on my bike to spend the day with Sylvie. It was August and the days were long. They would not expect me back till 10.30 or 11 p.m. Then they would start to worry, and I could visualize the discussion the three spinsters would have. Mademoiselle Thérèse, the strict one, hunching her thin shoulders and saying, "She should at least have let us know she was going to be so late." Then Mademoiselle Gabrielle saying placatingly, "But she has so little fun, I expect she's staying the night at Sylvie Feuillatte's flat." Mademoiselle Marie, who echoed her sisters' views alternately, would sigh and shake her head. Eventually, presumably, they would telephone the Feuillattes to reassure themselves –and then . . . I imagined them rushing up to my little room and finding the letter and – Oh! the shame of it struck me anew. They would be horrified.

I mustn't think about it too much, or I wouldn't have the courage to leave. I waved gaily and, calling, "*A ce soir*", wobbled off on my bike, trembling violently. I was to leave it at Titi's flat and she was going to accompany me in the train as far as Bordeaux. The incredible journey had now begun; my passport was left behind and I was now Marie Cornet, born in Lyons but resident in Paris with my parents, and off to see my aunt for the annual summer holiday.

The first time my identity card was checked by a guard I couldn't breathe. Surely my guilt must show, but apparently not. He checked my ticket and punched it, and I relaxed. It was a very long train journey from Paris to Bordeaux, but I thought of the previous one from Quimper to Besançon which took three days, and this seemed such a contrast, so comfortable in the second-class compartment and only taking one day. We didn't talk much. I was sleepy after the restless night and we might have said something which would have aroused suspicion.

Finally, after dark, we reached Bordeaux. It was stickily hot, being so much further south, and the two of us spent another restless night in company with several hundred mosquitoes in a small hotel. Next morning, the man who was going to direct me to the farm joined us in the lobby. He had been told that the older woman would hold a white handkerchief in her hand, so that he could identify us and greet us as if we were old friends. Titi was going back to Paris and left me in his safe hands. It was now up to me. The stranger explained to me that he would take my small suitcase in his farm van and drive with it, hidden under sacks, to the farmhouse. The land belonging to the "*passeur*" (someone who passed people from one side of the frontier to the other) lay on both sides of the border. In my usual foggy way, I had imagined a neat line cutting across fields, and roads, like a bit of tape: on one side German-occupied France and on the other the free zone. He also explained to me that, though the farmer's house was still in occupied France, the dreamt-of freedom lay two or three fields away on the other side. In order to allay suspicion in the little country lanes, I would be dropped off from the van and must then walk along a lane with only a basket over my arm.

We drove along in silence. The suspense was tremendous. As instucted, I got off when he stopped, thanking him casually for the lift, and walked along purposefully, though I hadn't a clue where I was going! Still, it would look suspicious if I appeared to be lost. Before I had time to worry unduly a person on a bicycle, whom I had been told to watch out for, passed me slowly and, about a hundred yards ahead, dropped a spare tyre he was carrying, dismounted to pick it up, nodded his head imperceptibly up a lane to the right and rode on. This was where I had to turn up to the farm and, if asked by German patrols who guarded the border fiercely, I was to say I was buying eggs from the farm as usual. My heart beat fast but all was quiet, and the little lane ended at a farm gate. I practically fell into the farmer's wife's arms, weeping with relief. They saw how tired I was, and how hungry! They knew I still had a long way to go and was pretty young, so they wisely made me eat a delicious casserole. I just couldn't stop eating. Then I was made to lie down in their feather bed to have a good sleep and recover my strength.

At lunchtime we had discussed the best time for me to cross over the fields into unoccupied France. It was generally felt that mid-afternoon would be safest. The heat made everyone sleepy, and it looked less suspicious than at dusk or at night. After a good hour's sleep, in the way of all the young, I felt fully rested and ready for the most frightening part. The farmer's wife dressed me in a voluminous, dark dress and ugly great shoes. She put an old hat on me, dirtied my face and hands, so I couldn't even recognize myself. She gave me a basket to carry, with my own shoes and washing things in the bottom and a layer of beans on the top. Then from a window she showed me where to cross the first field. In the distance I could see a gap in the hedge; I was to go straight through this, as though I did it every day of my life. If I saw the German guards patrolling in the next field, I was to appear to be weeding and, above all, on no account to walk hurriedly. Straight on across the second field, through a gate on to a little road and I would be safe. The farmer's friend would meet me there with the van and my little suitcase, my only luggage.

It was a baking hot day and, after thanking the farmer and his wife most deeply and kissing them goodbye, I set off. The heat and the fear made me drip with sweat, and my legs didn't seem to belong to me. I spoke sharply to myself: after all, even if they did arrest me they wouldn't shoot me. I was only a girl, and a useless one at that. Yet somehow at that moment I couldn't quite believe the logic of my reasoning. The field seemed enormous; the basket was heavy and the long skirt difficult to walk in. Up a little bank and through the hedge – my heart pounding, my mouth dry, all the classical clichés of terror. There was a slight rise in the middle of the second field, so I could not see the gate straightaway and nearly panicked. I tried not to look to right or left and wondered if, and when, and how, the patrol would appear, and how I would react – probably scream and run! I seemed to have been walking for an eternity when I saw the gate and, feeling I could now make it, relaxed a bit. Glancing to one end of the field I saw the patrol, lying on the grass fast asleep! I felt cheated – all that terror for nothing! The relief when I got to the road and started walking along it was indescribable. In no time at all the van appeared, I thumbed it as though cadging a lift, and the kind accomplice drove me to the little local station. I changed out of the "disguise" in the van, fished out my shoes and washing things, putting them back in my suitcase, and became Mademoiselle Marie Cornet again. The driver wished me *"Bonne Chance"* and was gone.

Over and over again, throughout the years to come, I marvelled at the cool courage of all the French men and women who helped me. The Resistance Movement has been written about in many books, particularly the way in which they smuggled airmen and underground Intelligence workers back to England. But that was a different matter. The men and women they helped were going back to fight the Germans again. It was a truly worthwhile risk. The people who helped me risked torture and death and put their families at risk – for what? For a young schoolgirl who could do nothing for the war effort, even if she did reach home; yet they did it cheerfully. I wondered if ordinary English people would have behaved in the same manner towards a French girl in my position. I like to think they would!

I was obliged to produce my *carte d'identité* at the station when I asked for a ticket to a nearby town, but with only French police around it didn't seem nearly so frightening. It was a real joy not to see the ugly Hun uniform and to feel FREE. I was drunk with the idea. I felt I could escape anywhere now. How premature and foolish of me!

At the town of Montauban I found out about trains to Grenoble and was able to get a sleeper for the main part of the journey. As I was now French, I was grateful for the fact that I spoke French like a Frenchwoman. I proffered my identity card with equanimity and stopped worrying, even when it was studied closely; my whole body was singing with freedom.

The train soon rocked me to sleep and I awoke to the glorious views of the country round Grenoble. Even in the middle of summer snow-capped mountains shimmered in the distance; it was all of a fairytale beauty and *no more Germans!*

Ruth was there to meet me in Grenoble, wearing a rose in her buttonhole so that I would recognize her. She greeted me affectionately and took me straight to a hotel for a good meal. The schoolgirl in me was starving again, not having eaten since the marvellous lunch on the previous day, just before the escape. Ruth was living in a little village not far from Grenoble, in a small hotel. We went there by bus, chatting easily and finding out about each other. Though we were both cousins of Diana Provost, we were not related to each other and had never met before. There was a lot of news to catch up on. She was in her forties, with chestnut hair and a kind face; she had never married. She had booked me a room in the hotel.

I felt I was walking on air, but the concentration and tenseness of the past few weeks had tired me mentally and physically and Ruth wisely suggested an early night. It was very sweet and comforting to have somone come and say goodnight and ask if I was comfy. Ruth's parting words were reassuring: "Sleep very tight and have a long lie-in. We'll have a lazy day tomorrow and I'll show you around." Breathing a deep sigh, sheer contentment poured over me and I slept deeply.

So deeply was I asleep that I didn't hear Ruth come into my room next morning long before 7 a.m. I imagined I was dreaming and turned over. Ruth's face

66

alarmed me: she looked horror-stricken and could hardly speak. The words tumbled out distorted with emotion and the tears she would not allow to fall: "Tonia, you've got to go. They're rounding up all the Jews in unoccupied France. There's no time. There's a bus outside and your name is on the list. The Germans are making the Vichy police arrest them. Tonia, so many Jews have escaped recently into the free zone that they have asked at all the hotels for recent arrivals, and they are certain you are a Jew. They're taking you away." She clasped me to her with a comforting hug. I was stunned and numb, with a sensation of stark sickening fear that I had never experienced before.

"How long have I got?" We stared at each other, misery in our eyes, the joy of yesterday wiped out. Never would I forget that instant.

Ruth answered, in tears, "Ten minutes. The bus is waiting for you. It's going to all the villages; and, Tonia, another tragedy has happened. The Duke of Kent has been killed in an air crash." We both cried unashamedly. Better to cry at an impersonal event.

I dressed hurriedly. I could take nothing with me except a bag. I thought, with awful finality, "Of course not. The Jews don't have long to live where they are sent." I clung to Ruth, and then the police came and pushed me into the bus. It was a heart-rending and shattering sight. The bus was already full of weeping Jews, men and women, mainly French Jews. They wrung their hands and clung to each other, the epitome of abject misery. I had to stand, fairly near the front, while the bus wound its way round the villages, picking up Jews in the market-places – known Jews, who had been rounded up, herded into the village squares, waiting for certain, horrible death. I could not feel sorry for myself any longer. I was appalled at what I saw. At one stop a woman in her thirties, standing with her three young children, was brutally wrenched away from them and forced into the bus. The children, screaming, tried to climb on to the bus with her and were pushed back. Then she went completely insane. Before our eyes she became a demented lunatic. She attacked everyone in the bus, clawing at our hair, our faces. Saliva dribbled from her mouth, and her eyes rolled and stared. Before the bus drove on I saw that a woman in the street was trying to hold and comfort the children, the youngest of which can only have been three. I tried to tell the poor mad mother that someone was looking after them, but she was too far gone. She screamed the whole way down to Grenoble in the bus, tearing up and down past the standing passengers – the most terrifying sight and sound of my life. In all the four and half years of my "useless war" this memory remained the most vivid, searing itself into my heart and soul. Never again would I be an unthinking girl. I aged to the end of time during that bus ride. At another village a man, dying of cancer, who had been taken from his bed, was allowed to have his wife to help him into the bus and ride with him down to Grenoble. She wasn't Jewish though, and when we reached the big iron gates of yet another barracks she had to leave him. They were old and they were resigned, with immense dignity, to an end they must have anticipated.

At the gates of the big French barracks many friends were waiting to shout encouragement and I saw, with deep gratitude and affection, that Ruth, too, had found out where this doomed race was being assembled. She shouted so that I could hear, "I shall do all in my power, at the Prefecture, to prove you are English and not Jewish. If it's possible, do something too and do it quickly. There isn't much time." By that she meant the trucks in the station yard, near to the barracks, which were already waiting, waiting to take us to certain death, waiting, filled with lime.

Inside the barracks there were hundreds, maybe thousands, of Jews. They huddled together in a wailing mass and I felt ashamed for them, and then ashamed at myself for feeling like that. After all I was crying too, but, I hoped, quietly. No Geneva Convention could help me now. The realization that I had not got the power and influence of the British Government behind me was devastating. I was a stateless, homeless, condemned Jewess. A young French soldier saw me standing apart from the crowd. He obviously felt sorry for me and asked if I had had anything to eat. By now it was mid-morning and, having had no breakfast, I *was* feeling hungry. He offered to get me something in his "*gamelle*" (a soldier's mess-tin). I ate what he brought me discreetly, otherwise, I felt, the whole crowd would engulf me. The soldier talked to me and this did wonders for my morale. I felt much better, even managing a tender, sad and, I was certain, a final flirtation.

Fortified by food, I decided I must do something. The soldier told me the Préfet himself was dealing with queries. The Préfet, I suppose would be the equivalent of the Chairman of the County Council. He took me to his office in a different part of the barracks. A long queue of gesticulating, hysterical men and women had already formed. I decided to provide a contrast and live up to the casual, off-hand, stiff-upper-lip attitude expected of the British. The Préfet was in a state of nervous exhaustion. His was a hideous role – to be forced by the Germans at long range to send French Jews off to concentration camps.

I spoke calmly but firmly, I hoped: "I am *not* a Jew. My name is LYON-SMITH, not Marie Cornet. I haven't got my passport because I left it behind in Paris when I escaped." He interrupted me wearily: "If you knew, Mademoiselle, of the number of people denying they are Jews this morning, you would have tried a different story." I was furious. It was the first time anyone had accused me point-blank of lying. I started to speak again, but he had already waved me on, and was dealing with the next in the queue. By now I was far more cross than frightened, determined to prove that I was English. I knew that the only way to achieve this would be to get the Préfet to ring through to the Commissariat in the Boulevard Jean Mermoz in Neuilly. They would confirm that an "Antonia Lyon-Smith" had indeed escaped from Paris. Back I went to the end of the queue so that I could put this to the Préfet. He was slightly surprised to see me again and was sarcastic about my request: "Perhaps you would like me to ring your parents too!" This was nearly too much for me to bear, and though I begged him to telephone Paris, he apologized, saying he was much too busy. The day seemed to be slipping by and already some Jews had been marched off to the station.

Once again I went to the back of the queue and once more came face to face with the harassed Préfet. "Not you again?" This time I was past caring what anyone thought about my manners and answered him icily, "I insist that you telephone Paris – and I think that if you don't you'll be jolly sorry at the end of the war." I waited, breathless at my audacity. I had never spoken to anyone like that. Suddenly he relented, promising he would get someone to verify my story. "Such a lie, it could possibly be true." He told me to go off and sit down. I felt drained, despairing. By now it was nearly 5 p.m. and the barracks was to be cleared of everyone by that evening. I wandered off and found a room where some foreign Jews (not French) were still gathered, speaking languages I couldn't understand. They asked me my nationality and could hardly believe it when I told them that I was English.

About an hour later one of the officials from the Préfet appeared and announced that all Estonian, Lithuanian, Latvian and American Jews were to be released. He didn't mention British, so I leapt to my feet and shouted "What about me?" He beckoned me to follow him through what was by now a largely deserted building. It was nearly 7 p.m. and the Préfet was alone. He *had* telephoned to Paris. The police in Neuilly hadn't noticed I hadn't been in to sign. I silently cursed my careful signatures for three days in advance! However, they had checked at the *pension*, found I was indeed missing and confirmed the genuine British passport left there. They had then 'phoned back to the Préfet in Grenoble. I could have hugged him. How incredibly lucky I was to have been born English. I thanked him warmly for the trouble he had taken. He looked drawn and pale. "There was *nothing* I could do for the others." His sorrow was painful to see.

Shaken and dishevelled, I walked out of the barrack gates, having escaped the most ignominious death of all, and wondered how I could get back to Ruth. But there was Ruth waiting for me! She had been telephoning too – everyone, the Préfet in the barracks, the police in Paris. All day she had pestered officials and fought for me. I clung to her, overcome and sobbing uncontrollably. I would never be carefree again and the nightmare haunted me for years.

VI
❦ Love in the Alps ❦

RUTH WISELY REALIZED that I was in a state of shock. Though I talked and acted normally, my whole body would suddenly tremble violently at the memory of what I had escaped. The thought of what my companions on that day were now undergoing turned my nights into nightmares, and I cried out in fear if I drifted back into sleep. For a week I was hardly aware of living at all. Ruth was gentle and kind: "We'll go to a little mountain village, called Uriage, just for a week or so, and we'll celebrate your 17th birthday there."

I had so little to pack and no dress cool enough for the heat of summer in the south of France. Ruth bought me a pretty summer skirt in gay colours and a cool green blouse. This was a great treat for me as I had been wearing school clothes for years now, or so it seemed. The short journey to Uriage, the excitement of a birthday, the lovely sunshine, all helped to make me forget. We had my birthday tea sitting at a little table outside in the sun.

Unfortunately I had other embarrassing troubles, but I finally plucked up my courage and said to Ruth, "I've got the most awful itching feeling down there, front *and* back. What shall I do?" Calmly and reasonably Ruth persuaded me to go to a doctor. This was an utterly mortifying experience. He asked me if I was a virgin. I blushed crimson. That anyone should think I *wasn't* at my age. I rounded on him with flashing eyes. He quietened me down and explained he would have to examine me, warning me that if I had never been examined before, it might be painful. He said that he thought I might have caught V.D., which, at the time, I had never even heard of. The examination, however, revealed the childish complaint of thread worms! How undignified! I suppose I must have caught them in the camp. Without proper medicines or treatment they proved very difficult to shift. We even tried the old French peasant's cure of a whole head of crushed garlic cloves boiled in milk and administered as an enema – too pungent to be tried more than once! The boils and carbuncles on my face reappeared and the poor doctor, with no antibiotics at his disposal, tried cauterizing them. This was done with a small instrument looking like a miniature firework sparkler. When it was red hot he seared the festering boil. It was agonizing if it touched good flesh, and I couldn't keep still. It didn't do much good anyway, as the burns went bad and took as long to heal as the boils did when poulticed and brought to a head. The really astonishing thing was that none of them in the end left permanent scars.

While all this was going on, various enquiries were being made about our slipping over the border into Spain or being repatriated. Ruth didn't want to leave, and she thought that the escape routes into Spain were too hazardous for me on my own. There were also fairly hair-raising reports of what happened to people when they actually reached Spain. Some were put into detention or "holding" camps for ages and forgotten about. Spain was determined to stay neutral, and not help anyone really. She had enough troubles of her own.

Ruth and I visited various Embassy officials in Grenoble who reckoned it was safer to do nothing. We therefore made plans for the winter. Ruth had spent the previous winter in a little hotel in the village of Lancey near Grenoble. She had two small rooms there, one as a bedroom and the other a tiny sitting room. It had a table and divan bed and two chairs. She sweetly insisted on me sleeping in the bedroom, while she took over the sitting-room.

The proprietor was a great character and an excellent cook. Like many good chefs, he drank rather a lot and one never quite knew what mood he was going to be in. The little hotel was used mainly by businessmen. Lancey had a huge paper-making factory and anyone connected with the enormous machines or the end product would come and stay there. Up in the mountains above Lancey there were huge generators transforming water from the dams into electricity. Ruth and I kept quietly to ourselves as we did not want to advertise the fact that we were English! Still, at mealtimes it was only natural to chat to the regular visitors to the Inn. One of them was an electrical engineer called Durand. He was in his thirties, a stocky young man, with fair curly hair, blue eyes and a wistful, worried look. He was friendly and kind, and would often talk to us and give us news of the outside world and the war. By the late autumn of 1942 the North African campaign was nearly over and the British had won many victories over Rommel. We learnt of Montgomery and the Eighth Army for the first time. Little did I know that my father, as C.R.A. Sixth Armoured Division, was instrumental in knocking out hundreds of German tanks. I still had no news of either of my parents, and by now was relieved that they had no idea of what was happening to me.

Ruth had a few books, but we had no wireless, no letters to write, nor anything to sew or knit. I was content to drift for a while. I was delighted once again to have no school but began to feel I should be learning something. I asked Durand if he could give me some maths lessons. He was only too pleased to do so, as he was very fond of me. Soon I became aware that it wasn't the maths I looked forward to. I would use some of Ruth's face powder, make myself as attractive as possible, and wait with fluttering heart for him to arrive with the books, and then ignore the maths and just talk to him endlessly, asking questions about what he did and where the electricity generating plants were. He would explain it all so carefully to me, but I could never understand the complexity of it all. I was selfishly and cruelly exploiting what I knew was happening. He was falling in love with me. One day he offered to take me in his little service van up to one of the hydros in the mountains. This was an exciting event, for we never went out, except for walks.

It was an astounding experience to see and hear the thunderous roar of the cascading torrents outside, contrasting with the utter silence, except for the hum of the turbines in the cavernous and spotless vaults, like cathedrals built into the mountainside. I was sincerely impressed, even if I could not begin to understand. On the way back down to Lancey I talked to him, the first time that I had actually talked about the tragic day in Grenoble, and it did me a lot of good, even though I was trembling by the time I had finished. Durand was appalled. He stopped the little van, taking my hands in his to stop the trembling. Then, very gently, and with infinite respect and gentleness he put his arm round me and laid my head on his shoulder. I relaxed and cried. When my tears had stopped, I started to say how sorry I was, but he stopped me: "Tony, *je vous aime*. I have loved you for weeks now. It is impossible. I love my wife too. I must leave Lancey as soon as I can without arousing suspicion, and stay somewhere else."

Though I had guessed at his feelings for some time, it made me so happy to hear him say it, and I couldn't bear the thought of him leaving me to the boredom of being on my own again – still as selfish as ever. I begged him not to leave the Inn. He kissed me on the lips, but such an innocent kiss.

It must be admitted that I behaved cruelly and disgracefully, but with a compulsive and yet innocent instinct that came from nowhere. I insisted on drawing his portrait, and achieved quite a good likeness. I was physically attracted by him, and loved the worried lines on his forehead, and the blue eyes which always looked so sad. His chin had a deep cleft in it, and his lashes were thick and fair. I even went to his room, feeling very daring, to do the portrait, and though aware of the effect I had on him, and myself excited by his presence, I could not know how much self-control he had to exert not to try to seduce me. He never did try. He adored me and I revelled in it. I should have been punished for my behaviour, and eventually I was, over and over again.

It was about this time, during the winter of 1942–1943, that Ruth told me a friend of her's was coming to stay. She was a bit embarrassed and upset at having to tell me. His name was Claude Spaak and Ruth had been a close friend of his, and his wife, Suzette, and their two children for many, many years. He was a playwright, and they lived in Paris. Usually Ruth lived with them in Paris, but since the German occupation she had been forced to come to the *zone libre*. They were all extremely fond of one another. I was abysmally ignorant of human emotions and was ashamed at not understanding the complexities and depths of different affections. At that age, seventeen, the young talk

76

endlessly among themselves about everything from sex to religion, but so far I had been too preoccupied with just existing, or escaping, to indulge in such discussions. In any case I had no one of my own age to talk to – no parties, no girl-friends, no parents, no healthy normal flirting at dances, no riding, no tennis. All my emotions were exaggerated and heightened by fear and danger. I was very lost.

Claude talked brilliantly, and I was fascinated. He stayed at the little hotel and I ate with them and even ventured to talk sometimes. He introduced me to the works of Pascal and Montaigne. I read Pascal's *Pensées* and Montaigne's essays and was moved and astounded at such a deep and bitter exposition of man's nature. I had been in limbo; now I had someone to admire. Claude was an atheist and, after my shattering experience with the Protestant Minister in Neuilly, I was sure Claude was right. There existed nothing but life itself. I was firmly converted to atheism. How very boring I must have been with my newly acquired philosophy, and learning; yet Ruth and Claude were patient and gentle with me and included me in their conversations.

The snows came and it was bitterly cold as 1942 froze into 1943. Claude went back to Paris, but before he left he and Ruth worked out a plan for the two of us to cross over the Swiss border near Lake Annecy. We knew that this would be a much more arduous escape than from occupied France into the free zone. It was midwinter and there would be a long and hard climb over icy, snow-blocked mountain tracks. On the other hand the police, knowing this, relaxed their vigil on the mountain passes during the rigorous winter months.

One bitter morning, with the temperature well below freezing, we dressed warmly and with only a small suitcase each, caught the bus to Grenoble, and from there another one to Chambéry. At the bus depot in Chambéry we found one going to the little village in the mountains where we would be taken to the house of the *passeur* who, for a hefty fee, was to guide us over the frontier into Switzerland. Ruth and I looked very conspicuous in that local bus full of peasants and farmers. There was a hostile atmosphere. No one spoke to us, and the long and tiring journey passed in silence. The atmosphere when we reached the last village was equally inhospitable. People glanced at us and quickly looked the other way. We began to feel distinctly unwelcome as we asked several people the way to the *passeur's* house, nearly two kilometres out of the village. We reassured each other by saying it was only natural for them to be suspicious; there might be people wanting to get addresses in order to receive money for the information. By the time we reached the house we were wet and cold and tired. We knocked and the *passeur* let us in furtively. He looked pretty untrustworthy, but by this time there was little we could do about it.

It was late afternoon and our bus rides had started before dawn, so we were hungry too! The man suggested a bowl of soup while we discussed how we would cross over, and exactly what to do. He also said it would be safer to pay him now, rather than wait for a possible patrol to intercept us. If that should happen he would slip quietly back and, as we were women, it was unlikely that we would be shot at and we could always pretend we were "going it alone". His behaviour did not inspire us with confidence, but we were powerless to back out now. Ruth had paid him and we were deciding what time of night we should start out when the sound we had been dreading made us jump, our hearts in our mouths. There was a loud pounding on the door. The *passeur* didn't seem surprised or worried,

78

which made us suspicious, and when he opened the door there were two French Vichy policemen. It was obvious that "informers" had denounced us as we got off the bus in the village. Quite possibly they got a rake-off too from the *passeur*, who had neatly acquired the money before the police arrived. Ruth and I didn't think of all this at the time. We were heartbroken at having got so near the border.

We were driven to the police station in Chambéry where the long interrogation began. The policeman was bored and had nothing to do, so he proceeded to take down our life stories – in longhand! It took hours; but he did end up feeling sorry for us, and the atmosphere became much more friendly as soon as he realized that we were British. It was warm in the office, and we were given a delicious crusty chunk of French bread with ham and butter. Obviously the police knew how to look after themselves! As it was now about 9 p.m. Ruth and I began wondering where on earth we would be spending the night, and presumed it would be in a police cell at the station. However, much to our astonishment and unbelievable relief, the police said we could go free! Provided we didn't try to escape again! They also offered to drive us to a hotel in Chambéry for the night. It was a fairy-tale ending!

Ruth and I were highly amused to find we had been given a room next to a high-ranking German officer who was spending a few days' leave there. Had he but known that his next-door companions were two British women! Obviously we did *not* speak English.

Next day we toured the town like a couple of tourists before returning to Lancey. The proprietor and guests at the little hotel were astounded to see us and could hardly believe our story: "We presumed you would either be in Switzerland or in a French jail." "So did we!" we replied.

We were happy to settle back into a routine existence. I went for long walks along the farm tracks. Occasionally I persuaded a farmer to sell me some farm butter, goat cheese or fresh milk. There were many walnut trees in that district, and I picked quite a few. We blended the nuts with the soft fresh goat cheese which made a delicious mixture.

Durand was not there all the time, as he had other districts to visit and electrical equipment to maintain elsewhere. I was very relieved, especially as a most unusual young man was now staying at the hotel. His name was Daniel Héry. He was very tall for a Frenchman, his hair was cut "en brosse" (very short) and he was extremely ugly, with a scar above one eye which pulled it down at the corner – but he was utterly fascinating. Ostensibly he was there to study the machinery at the paper factory. His father made these vast machines and he was making a detailed study of them. Each one varied according to what was fed into it to make the paper. The one at Lancey took in wood, rags, cardboard or rubbish generally.

Daniel was fun. His approach to life was lighthearted and amusing. I had nearly forgotten what it was like to laugh at things, to make fun of people and be treated as a grown-up. He had immense charm and treated me gently. I began to hero-worship him, and used to copy out his notes for him tidily, and trace the complicated drawings of machine parts. It amused him that I so enjoyed doing this for him. When he spoke English, it was with a strong American accent which I thought very funny. Ruth liked him too and, though we sat at different tables for our meals, occasionally we would have our "ersatz" coffee together. Sometimes, though, he would be very moody and not talk to anyone, and I soon learnt to respect this and not to interrupt. I think he

80

was studying "company law" as well. He took me down to the factory. It was very noisy, but fascinating to watch the whole process from start to finish: all the rubbish composed of wood, rags and so on, churning round in huge vats at one end, and at the other end of this vast machine, which seemed to stretch for miles, long cylindrical rolls of paper would appear as if by magic. I thought it the cleverest thing I had ever seen.

When Durand came back for occasional visits to the nearby generators, he met Daniel and realized, before I did myself, that I was beginning to love this tormented and strange young man. He was naturally jealous, but was such a genuinely kind and thoughtful country person that he wanted to protect me from what he feared Daniel, as a Parisian, might be and do. I wouldn't listen to his gently given advice. By now, even though I was slightly frightened of Daniel, I loved him deeply. I wasn't "in love" with him – he was so strange, occasionally so distant and cynical about everything, sometimes quite cruelly, sometimes more gently. I had no idea at this time of his background, even whether he was married or not. To me he seemed old at twenty-seven – ten years older than me. Occasionally I wondered why he wasn't fighting somewhere.

About this time Ruth decided that it would be safe for her to go to Paris for a short while to stay with the Spaaks. She used a false French identity card for the journey, which was usually sufficient for a trouble-free trip. She felt I knew everyone by now and would not be lonely without her. She wouldn't be away for more than a few weeks.

It was extremely bad luck that I got a very bad attack of tonsilitis a few days after Ruth left. I had a very high temperature and couldn't swallow. Daniel had promised Ruth he would look after me and this he proceeded to do very efficiently. He got the doctor for me, but he could do little except prescribe poultices on the neck and chest, inhaling a herbal mixture, and cold compresses on the forehead to reduce the burning heat and ache in my head. There was no penicillin, of course. I was very ill and delirious. Daniel nursed me with the gentleness of a mother. Each day he brought me cool drinks, and put the steaming mustard poultices on my neck and chest. My throat was thickly covered with white spots and I felt ghastly.

For over a week I lay there, alternately shivering and sweating, hardly aware of the devoted care Daniel took of me. He made my bed, changed my nighty, washed me, and did it all as though I were a little girl. It was then he started to call me *"Mon petit lapin"*. As I slowly got better and the fever dropped, I became aware of all he had done for me. I was deeply ashamed of the nuisance I must have been, of all the time he must have spent looking after me when he should have been studying. My gratitude and admiration overwhelmed me and, one evening when he brought my small supper up to me, I told him how much I loved and admired him. He quietly told me I *mustn't* love him, that he wasn't at all a worthy person. How could I believe that, in view of all the menial tasks he had performed for me, more skilfully and more lovingly than any trained nurse? He did his best to stop me loving him, but he felt sorry for me and knew I must be in need of love. For the past two years I had been deprived of family love, neither able to give nor receive it. Then he kissed me. No one had kissed me like that for two years, not since the disgraceful episode with Egon Martin. This time I kissed with love; tenderness, happiness and complete confidence filled my whole being. Later on, when I was fully recovered, he wanted to make love to me – he had never told me he loved me but I knew he was very fond of me – but when he realized I was a virgin he immediately stopped caressing me. I adored him so much, I felt sure he would ask me to marry him one day. Meanwhile he brought books back from Paris on his infrequent trips there. I read most of Balzac and some of Thomas Hardy, quite beautifully translated into French. The modern authors seemed hard and cynical, but then so was Voltaire, so was Rabelais. Daniel would listen patiently to my enthusiastic and youthful philosophizing.

The spring came as an enchantment. Daniel seemed to spend a lot of time in Lancey. Unfortunately he disliked Claude and thought him affected and pedantic, but he was fond of Ruth and so managed to be polite to the admittedly rather self-satisfied "author". Daniel and I would go on long hikes, right up into the mountains round Lancey – stiff climbs to a pass or col where the views were quite breathtaking – a sheer drop through pine forests down to green fields full of mountain flowers, with the shining ribbon of the river Isère in the far distance, winding through a fairy-tale landscape. Further on still, more mountains, snow-capped. In April the sun was burning hot and the sky a violent blue. Daniel would make me take my shirt off and eventually I stopped being shy and would strip to the waist. It was an unbelievable sensation, like swimming naked, which I had done as a child in the lake at my grandfather's house. I had never thought of my figure, except to wish I could be nearly flat-chested. Daniel would stroke me very gently, and was the first person to tell me that my figure was beautiful. We also discovered an old château, the Château de Lancey, high above the village, about four or five kilometres away. It was deserted, enchanting, straight out of Grimm, with round turrets at the four corners and, in the front, a wide stone terrace with a balustrade. From this overhanging terrace there was a steep drop, and the same glorious view of the Isère valley. Sometimes I would go up there on my own with a book, or a drawing board and my pastels. I like pretending the château belonged to me. I gave the pastel of it to Daniel.

One day in May I could bear it no longer.

"Daniel," I said, "I love you so much and you are happy with me. We laugh together and you enjoy being with me. *Please*, won't you marry me?" He was infinitely touched, but explained that he couldn't possibly.

"*Je t'aime bien, mon petit lapin*, but . . .", and he told me that apart from the difference in our ages, the war and the fact that I had met no one else, and though he did enjoy my sense of humour, my intelligence, and my beauty, I was not "*douce*". It is an impossible word to translate into English. It really means a gentle, loving nature that accepts all adversities quite calmly, and is kind to everyone, both *to* them and behind their backs. He then told me that for many years he had in fact loved a girl who was all these things, but who would not marry him; and this was why he was still, at twenty-seven, unmarried. Though this made me desperately unhappy and I cried, I understood and was deeply grateful for having known such a man. Our relationship remained unchanged, and if I did ask him to marry me again, it was only in fun. He was a sick man already, and though many years after the war he did eventually marry the woman he had loved for so long, it was a short-lived happiness for he died of cancer soon afterwards in his forties.

Now another young man appeared at the small hotel, very dark and good-looking and rather pleased with himself. He was involved with the factory. His father had a factory somewhere that made cardboard boxes. For him, when he met me, for some inexplicable reason it was a *"coup de foudre"*. Daniel was back in Paris and Ruth was either writing to Claude, or he was down in Lancey visiting her, so I was only too happy to be taken out by this handsome young man, Gérard Lourdelet. I was still very much in love with Daniel but I presumed that a lighthearted flirtation would hurt no one. During the end of May and June we got to know each other well. He was possessive and jealous and I was flattered by this. Living from day to day, thinking endlessly about my parents, when I would see them again, and when the war would end, I welcomed any diversion. The heat of early summer became oppressive in the valley, and there seemed no room, no privacy, no air in the tiny rooms in the hotel in Lancey. Apart from our bedrooms there was only the dining-room to sit in.

Gérard would take me to a restaurant in Grenoble occasionally, which made me feel very sophisticated. I still didn't wear any make-up, which would be un-thinkable in a seventeen-year-old these days. I became tanned very easily and, though I had no pretty clothes to ring the changes with, I suppose I looked attractive as all the young do, with a tall, slim figure.

Then Daniel came back from Paris, met Gérard and disliked him intensely. He warned me that he was a conceited, selfish young man, with which I agreed. It pleased me that he minded and I thought it might make him jealous. I therefore pretended to fall in love with Gérard, who thought he was in seventh heaven and promptly asked me to marry him. Without really thinking of the consequences I kissed him as though I meant it and murmured, "Yes".

That night I thought how dreadfully badly I was behaving. First of all there was Peter Dougall in St. Denis internment camp, who was firmly convinced I was going to marry *him*. As neither of us could write to the other, I had selfishly put him to the back of my mind, and quite honestly was hoping that the war would sort it all out somehow; and anyway we had only been fifteen and sixteen.

More recently, though, I had actually asked Daniel to marry me, and I really did love *him*. It was hard to say no to Gérard, which was why I had agreed, so I hoped once again that the war would sort things out and I wouldn't have to go through with any marriage. I asked Gérard to keep it a secret from Ruth, as well as from his family in Paris for the time being, making the excuse that I couldn't tell my own parents! He was perfectly content with that reasoning. However, what I hadn't reckoned on, because it had never happened before, was the physical revulsion I felt for him when he tried to kiss me too passionately. I found this very hard to conceal. Eventually I had to ask Ruth's advice.

"It's all my fault. I should never have said I would marry him. It's all such a mess. What *shall* I do?"

Ruth saw my real distress and, sympathetic as always, told me I must break it off. I was horrified.

"Ruth, *you* tell him. Tell him I'm too young to know my own mind. It would be better coming from you. Say you forbid it."

Ruth was, quite rightly, adamant. "That would be cowardly. No, you must do it yourself."

How and when could I do it? I was slightly afraid of him because he had an uncontrollable temper and would be devastated by my breaking off our engagement only a few weeks after accepting him. He began to suspect something was wrong when he noticed that I did my best not to find myself alone with him. He would demand explanations, gripping my wrist until it hurt. As I was so cowardly I kept giving in, until in desperation I fixed on a day and arranged that it should happen in Grenoble where there would be so many people around that he couldn't possibly do anything violent. Gérard was thrilled at the idea of taking me to Grenoble again and having me all to himself for lunch. He told me we would visit a jeweller in the afternoon and he would buy me a ring. I was helpless and had to feign rapture, while feeling a complete traitor. The whole situation was far too complicated to deal with. A straightforward war was much easier to cope with. With escaping or prison camp you knew where you were; decisions were made for you; you didn't have to think and emotion didn't come into it. I dreaded thinking about the day in Grenoble, feeling sick at what I was about to do. Yet I couldn't bear the thought of missing the superb lunch. It didn't even affect my appetite, so greedy and heartless was I. As it was a "special day" we had lunch in one of the best hotels – "Truite Grenobloise" and a delicious bottle of Chablis. Gérard even ordered, as an extra, wild strawberries. Their scent was overwhelming; I ate them with relish, yet guiltily. Even now they always remind me of that day. Steeling myself for what I had to do, I said, "Let's go somewhere cool for a walk, before going shopping." This was a mistake, for he readily agreed, thinking we might find a deserted corner of a park where he could kiss me. We went to just such a spot and, feeling like a murderess I told him, with the usual clichés, "I can't marry you. I know your parents will want you to marry a French girl, who will love you as you should be loved, and who would be far more worthy of your love than me", or words to that effect. His rage and anguish were terrifying. I thought he was going to hit me. Clenching his fists he walked away, then came back saying of course I didn't mean it. When the look in my eyes told him I did, he hissed obscene threats at me, accusing me of leading him on, etc., which was, I felt, rather true. The incident which seemed to upset him most, and which he kept raging about incoherently, was the fact that I had let him order wild strawberries when I knew what I was going to do to him. This nearly made me laugh. What a lucky escape I'd had! How fundamentally mean he must be to be able to think about such a detail. But of course I assured him that each mouthful had made me choke, and then, wickedly, offered to pay for them. I had no money, but I enjoyed saying it. He waved his arms in the air and looked as if he was about to explode. I waited dumbly. Then I saw he was crying, I longed to comfort him but I had to stop myself or I might have found myself engaged to him all over again. He implored me to "think over my decision", said he couldn't bear to see me for the time being and rushed away, head bent. I felt compassion and relief, but mostly relief, and heartlessly longed to tell Daniel about the wild strawberries, at the same time aware of the fact that I wanted to *prove* I wasn't *douce*. I found my own way back to Lancey, told Ruth it was all over and then promptly burst into tears myself.

By the summer of 1943 the Germans were in control of the free zone in France and had disarmed the Vichy French forces.* This happened shortly after my emotional upheavals and provided the right background of conjecture and worry as to what would happen to those British citizens who until now had remained unmolested. Gérard was still heartbroken, but genuinely fond enough of me to be worried – and rightly. It must

---

* They had actually occupied the free zone on 11th November, 1942.

Myself – Brittany 1939.

Diana Provost and me –
Nanny in
the background.

My cousin Diana
Provost, myself and
Diana's daughter Micky
(leaping) on the beach at
Concarneau.

Nanny (Victoria Jeynes),
myself and my little cousin
Micky at the Provosts'
house – behind us is the
aviary.

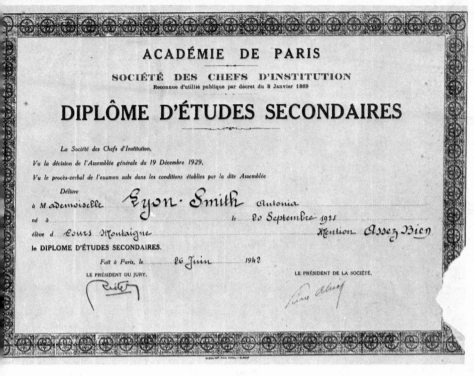

ACADÉMIE DE PARIS

SOCIÉTÉ DES CHEFS D'INSTITUTION
Reconnue d'utilité publique par décret du 8 Janvier 1869

DIPLÔME D'ÉTUDES SECONDAIRES

La Société des Chefs d'Institution,

Vu la décision de l'Assemblée générale du 19 Décembre 1929,

Vu le procès-verbal de l'examen subi dans les conditions établies par la dite Assemblée

Délivre

à Mademoiselle *Lyon-Smith* Antonia

né à _____ le 20 Septembre 1925

élève d *Cours Montaigne* _____ Mention Assez Bien

le DIPLOME D'ÉTUDES SECONDAIRES.

Fait à Paris, le 26 Juin 1942

LE PRÉSIDENT DU JURY,

LE PRÉSIDENT DE LA SOCIÉTÉ,

My diploma.

...ore this off the calendar on the ...sk in Room 333, 11 Rue des ...ussaies, Paris – Headquarters of ...e Gestapo. It was midnight and ...ey were all arguing about what ...do with me.

The address of the blond German secretary who was so kind to me and took me up to wash my hands each morning when she came on duty even after her home had been bombed and her family killed.

Berlin – Kaulsdorf
Hönowerstr. 23.

After my arrest, a suitcase was forwarded to me with this label attached to it. It contained among other things, my teddy bear – who was ripped to pieces by the Germans looking for secret messages. A truly heroic end, even unique – for a teddy bear.

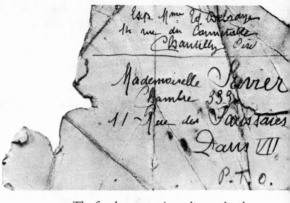

The food coupons issued to me by the Gestapo after I was released from solitary confinement because of illness, and placed under house arrest.

On the verso (*below*) is a prematurely sarcastic pro-German bit of propaganda. Translation:

"Newspaper cutting of 7th January 1944. Churchill states: 'Before the middle of March the world will witness one of the greatest military enterprises that history has ever known' – the soldier is saying: 'Shall I go? Shan't I? . . . Shall I? If I *don't* go, what will Stalin say? If I *do* go, what will Hitler do to me? Never mind, I shan't go!'"

I pinched this off the desk in Room 333, 11 Rue des Saussaies, Headquarters of the Gestapo in Paris, on the day of my release after five months' solitary confinement.

Der Kommandeur
der Sicherheitspolizei und des SD

in Paris · He/Kch.

B. Nr. Abtlg. IV P 4-614

Bitte in der Antwort vorstehendes Geschäftszeichen und Datum anzugeben.

Paris, den 22. Juli 1944
Rue de Saussaies 11
Fernsprecher: Anj 1404/7

An

Frl. Antonia Lyon-Smith,
17, rue Casimir,
Paris (7)

Betr.:

Bezug:

Anlagen:

Sie erhalten hiermit die Berechtigung in Paris
unter obiger Anschrift zu wohnen. Das Departement Seine dürfen
Sie nur mit hiesiger Genehmigung verlassen. Ausserdem haben Sie
als britische Staatsangehörige bei dem für Ihre obige Wohnung zu-
ständigen Polizeikommissariat der täglichen Meldepflicht nachzu-
kommen.
Dieses Schreiben haben Sie dem Polizeikommissariat sofort zur
Kenntnis vorzulegen.

Im Auftrage:

ß-Untersturmführer

BdS. I/II A — Nr. 263 — 20000

This is the other letter given to me after my release from 5 months' solitary confinement. Translation:
"The Commander of the Security Police and the S.D., 11 Rue des Saussaies in Paris.
With this you have the right to live in Paris at No. 17 Rue Casimir. You may only leave the Department of the Seine with permission from this office. In addition, as a British subject you must report daily to the Police Commissariat at your above place of residence. This letter is to be presented to the Police Commissariat immediately by order of:

S. S. Untersturmführer"

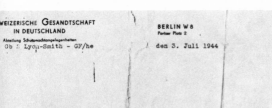

SCHWEIZERISCHE GESANDTSCHAFT
IN DEUTSCHLAND
Abteilung Schutzmachtangelegenheiten
Gb Lyon-Smith - GF/he

BERLIN W 8
Pariser Platz 2

den 3. Juli 1944

S C H U T Z B R I E F - 1944/67 GB

Die Schweizerische Gesandtschaft, Abteilung
Schutzmachtangelegenheiten, bescheinigt hiermit, dass

Fraeulein Antonia LYON-SMITH,

deren mit Unterschrift versehenes Lichtbild unten-
stehend angebracht ist, die britische Staatsangehoerig-
keit besitzt und somit unter schweizerischem Schutz steht.

Dieser Schutzbrief hat bis zum 3. Juli 1945 Gueltig-
keit.

SCHWEIZERISCHE GESANDTSCHAFT
Abteilung Schutzmachtangelegenheiten

One of the letters given to me when I was living under house arrest, after being released from the Gestapo, who were leaving Paris for Germany on the date at the top of the letter.
Translation:
"Letter of Safe Conduct. 1944/67GB
   "The Swiss Embassy, Section for Protective Matters, herewith certifies that Miss Antonia Lyon-Smith is a British subject and therefore is under Swiss protection. This letter of Safe Conduct is valid until 3rd July 1945."
This was sent from the Swiss Embassy in Berlin.

7th ARMOURED Div.

30

HEADQUARTERS
ROYAL ARTILLERY,
7th ARMOURED DIVISION,
HOME FORCES. BLA

7th ARMOURED Div.

The bearer of this note is
my daughter, Antonia Lyon-
Smith — she has been in
occupied France since 1940,
& has just been rescued from
Paris —
I would be grateful of any
assistance anyone can give
her in helping her to rejoin
her mother at Ayr, Scotland.

HEADQUARTERS Lyon Smith Brigadier
7th ARMOURED R.A. 7th Armoured Div.

[T. LYON-SMITH, BRIGADIER]

A letter from my father which was my sole means of identification on my return to England by Mosquito in August 1944. British Intelligence did not like this and had a sneaking suspicion I was a spy!

Self-explanatory if inaccurate in content.

To Civil and Military Police

27 Aug 44
Paris

This will identify Miss Antonia Lyons Smith
Her Father is Brigadier Lyons Smith of 2 British Corps.
She has been forced to remain in Paris during the
occupation, staying with her Canadian Cousin Mrs Marcel
Provost. Her father Brigadier Lyon Smith asked the
undersigned to try and locate Antonia. I shall advise
her father of her present location. I have instructed
Antonia to remain in Paris for a few days until the
Red Cross or British Legation or Civil affairs can
arrange for repatriation. She is to keep in touch with
Capt Cassills at the Canadian National Railways office
on the Rue Scribe.

Richard Malone
Lt Col
Canadian A.D.P.R. 21 Army Gp

Specimen Signature

Antonia Lyon Smith

CHIEF CONSTABLE'S OFFICE
6 SEP 1944
BURGH OF AYR

Liberation – Leclerc
arrives in Paris.

And so does De Gaulle seen outside Notre Dame.

Some less fleet-footed Germans were caught, rounded up and corralled in the Metro.

Victory euphoria is caught short by German snipers – Paris 1944.

Myself and friends – Devon 1981.

have been at the end of July or thereabouts that "an order" was served on Ruth and me "inviting" us – no less – to present ourselves at the barracks in Grenoble on such and such a date – complete with suitcase! What a very different approach to the terrifying snatching of the Jews the summer before. This time Ruth and I would be going together, and might possibly be sent to join Nanny, though of course we had no idea where she was, and presumed it was still Besançon. It seemed strange to be invited of one's own free will to give oneself up, but there was no alternative and a polite summons deserved an equally well-mannered accept · ance.

A grand farewell dinner was planned for the night before we left. The owner of the hotel, who was also a first rate chef, was giving it for us. Like everyone else he was really sad at the thought of our leaving for good. We were part of the family. About twenty attended that party, and Durand, Daniel and Gérard had a truce. It was a memorable and gargantuan meal. There must have been ten or fifteen courses, and the old man must have scoured the countryside and used up all his reserves to produce such riches. His best bottles of Burgundy were opened too. Everyone got very emotional towards the end; long-lasting pledges of friendship were made and the four-hour feast ended with a *bombe glacée*, all the ingredients of which were "unobtainable"! He even produced real coffee. We drunkenly and tearfully sang the *Marseillaise* but didn't dare to sing "God save the King" in case it got the hotel and other guests into trouble. Everyone had slight "hangovers" in the morning! Ruth and I thought lunchtime would be a good time to turn up at the barracks, and we caught the bus as if we were going on holiday. Daniel and Gérard even came with us to carry our bags, and see us installed. We all kissed each other goodbye at the entrance and the gates clanged to behind us.

To me the contrast between my last visit to this same barracks and the present round-up was indescribably different. The English and British people now affected were those who had been living mainly on the south coast, from Biarritz to Cannes. They were well dressed and well spoken, and completely casual about the whole situation. Old friends greeted one another with studied nonchalance:

"Bit different to the bar in Antibes, what?"

"Come and share our suite on the first floor!"

Their sense of humour, calm and phlegm impressed me all the more vividly as I recalled the cries and weeping of the huddled condemned Jews in that same building only a year ago.

There were straw mattresses in the rooms – two long rows facing each other, backed by another two rows. No segregation of the sexes. They were mostly husbands and wives anyway and nobody minded. They all seemed terribly old to me.

Once they were all settled, the various big rooms took on a civilized look. Mirrors were hung up; pretty scarves fluttered, expensive scent wafted exotically and no one seemed worried or upset. The French soldiers in the barracks were given big tips by the wealthier inmates to buy wine and extra titbits to liven up the meals served in the vast dining hall.

No one slept much the first night. Endless wisecracks floated out of the dark:

"I shan't put on my chiffon nightie; the straw will tickle."

"I shall never complain about the beds in Arles or Avignon again."

"I seem to be sharing *my* bed with a lot of tiny strangers!"

"Hold the mirror for me, darling, and the torch, while I take off my make-up."

"Remind me to talk to someone in the morning about the plumbing, there's no hot water!"

No one minded. The only way to wash was in the communal ablution block and in the morning all the men were busy shaving in cold water, and dressing neatly as though they were going shopping, or for a drive to some expensive coastal resort. Their spirit, in extremely uncomfortable surroundings such as they had never known in their lives, especially at their age, was very touching and very praiseworthy. I was proud to be British. I found one other young girl whose mother was French, but whose Father was British, and we became friends. It was fun to meet someone young. The camp was overcrowded and it was very hot. We wandered over to the main gates. What a surprise! There were Daniel and Gérard. They had wangled their way in past the French sentry on duty by telling him the girl they loved was inside. All the French are susceptible to love stories and they appeared so disconsolate that he asked them in and said they could stay for lunch. It was like something out of a comic opera. Ruth was delighted to see them too, and we all had a hilarious lunch with the other inmates. Daniel had brought some wine and the meal was a sort of cassoulet, not bad at all, but quite a contrast to the farewell dinner at Lancey. The two men spent the afternoon touring the camp and thinking of ways of escaping! We sat on a wall in the sun, chatting to various people and trying to find out how long we were going to be held in Grenoble, where we were going and so on.

One of the inmates was a delightful Irish priest, Father O'Hara. He kept going to see the Commandant of the camp in order to reassure some of the more elderly and worried British. Some were undergoing treatment, some had left animals or relatives behind. It was a strange situation because, although the Germans were in the camp offices, the guarding was done by Vichy French forces.

As many readers will remember, it was in September, 1943, that the Italian Defence Zone between the Rhône and the Alps was taken over by the Germans, and the Italian 4th Army was disarmed. It was at this time that the Italians became our allies. The situation was extremely confused.

The young girl, Lisette, and I became thoroughly domesticated and washed out our smalls in the big ablution block. We decided to come down after "lights out", when we could have the place to ourselves and have a really good wash. It was high summer so cold water didn't matter. We were too modest to strip in front of the dear old ducks, who would have been fearfully shocked. Accordingly, on the second or third evening we tiptoed downstairs and turned the lights on in the bare concrete washroom. We were splashing about naked, washing our feet in the stone troughs, when we heard a great roar of approval and laughter mingled with clapping coming from outside. We were horrified. It was, of course, pitch dark outside, and all the soldiers, seeing one brightly lit set of windows, had congregated gleefully and had been watching us while we washed. Mortified and blushing crimson, we hastily grabbed our towels and put out the lights. A good-natured groan went up from the men and we dashed back to our rooms.

Durand came to see us on the fourth day, which cheered us up. The novelty of being shut in had begun to wear off. He looked worried and said the Italians and Germans were disagreeing over the detention of the British in the newly-occupied free zone. He wondered what the outcome would be and hoped we weren't in danger. That very night when we were in bed we heard sounds of fighting and shooting outside the barracks and wondered what on earth was going on. Lisette and I were among the first downstairs and out on the barrack square at dawn, so we were possibly the first to see a truly magnificent and theatrical episode. The camp gates were flung open and a very handsome Italian officer in a flowing cape and a feather in his Robin Hood hat strode in and told us we were all free to leave. Just like that! They had had an "altercation" with the Germans in the night over this issue. The Italians had won, they were "on our side" now and they were in charge of that area of unoccupied France, or that was what we understood. No one had seen Italians in uniform before. Lisette and I embraced him warmly, thanked him effusively for "liberating" us, promised to start learning Italian straight away, and dashed back to tell everyone the crazy end of their short-lived captivity – four days of comic opera. Soon the news was relayed over a loudspeaker system and, without any more ado, the phlegmatic British packed their bags and left for home. The big joke was the fact that the Italians had actually *won* an argument.

"Must be the first battle they've ever won," everyone said.

Ruth and I happily returned yet again to the comfort of the little Lancey hotel rooms. The heat that August was really oppressive, so Ruth decided to move out of the valley and spend a few weeks in St. Pierre de Chartreuse, very near the famous monastery.

St. Pierre de Chartreuse was enchanting. It was fairly high up and surrounded by pine forests which produced a freshness and a scent of pine needles in the sun which was intoxicating. Claude came to stay there too. I was more lonely as Daniel couldn't come over very often and I began to wonder if the war would ever end. I thought constantly of Churchill and de Gaulle, the only names I knew of, as there was no news, either from newspapers or the wireless which nobody admitted listening to. I pinned all my hopes on them, and on my parents who assumed heroic and remote places in my thoughts. I so wanted to be worthy of them. The Résistance became known to me through various stories about them. They and their families were constantly being taken as hostages by the Germans because of railways and factories being sabotaged; then they would be tortured and shot. I did so wish I could do something useful, but I had no idea how to set about it and Ruth pointed out to me that she was responsible for me to Diana, and through her to my parents, so there was no question of any daring deeds. I walked in the mountains in the glorious sun, singing the charming old traditional French songs Daniel had taught me, and I read a lot in my sunny room but I was lonely and bored with drifting. It wasn't to last long.

Towards the end of August I began to feel ill, with a sore throat and splitting headache. For two days I lay in bed wishing Nanny was there, and the next morning I woke up covered in red spots – a good old-fashioned attack of measles. A doctor came, an extremely kind young man, a Belgian. His name was De Joncker. He was sympathetic and understanding and would stay and talk to me for ages. He felt sorry for me and was fond of me, and took me to a couple of parties when I was better. He was working for the Résistance, though he didn't talk about it much. What he did tell me was, indirectly, the cause of the only really gruelling period of my odd war. He told me that, should I need hiding, or false papers, or food coupons, he could arrange it for

Ruth and me. I was deeply grateful and promised to remember this, also telling Ruth and Claude about his kind offer. In the meantime both Ruth and Claude had decided that the Germans were behaving worse every day, as they began to realize that they were losing the war. They might easily take it out on any British citizen, whatever age or sex, and one could hardly rely on the Italians doing another "Sir Galahad" act!

Deportations were taking place every day and stories of terrifying tortures of the Gestapo had filtered through to the remotest villages. No one was safe. Claude decided that Ruth and I should acquire false identification papers (the second time for me) and go back to Paris separately and live inconspicuously with some French family as paying guests.

VII
☙ Prisoner of the Gestapo ❧

RUTH AND I discussed what names we would have on
our new false identity papers. I thought it might be a
help at least to have the same initials, and eventually
chose Antoinette Louise Savier. If I was going to live
with a family and be called by my Christian name all the
time Antoinette was very like Antonia.

I now learned for the first time that Durand was
connected with the Résistance; it was he who procured
the very professionally made identity cards. I saw him
one last time before leaving Lancey. We knew we
would never meet again and there was a finality and
sadness about our last few days at the little hotel which
had been home to Ruth and me for so long. Daniel was
already back in Paris, so I hoped I might see him
sometimes. I couldn't bear to part with the precious
books I had acquired, and there seemed to be a lot of
luggage, which included my teddy bear.

Ruth and I invented a story to go with my name and
decided that my father had been French-Canadian and
was dead, that my French mother was still in the South
of France. I would ad-lib the rest as and when questions
cropped up. The train journey back to Paris was fairly
uneventful. Having already presented false papers to
railway inspectors and policemen two years ago, it
didn't seem so terrifying this time, and anyway I was
nearly eighteen, very much older and wiser than the
sixteen-year-old who had coped before, or so I thought!

Quite recently my cousin Diana had had to leave her house in Concarneau as the Germans had occupied the whole of it. She had moved to a flat in Paris with her husband, Marcel, and her daughter Micky. The flat was in the Rue Casimir Périer, opposite the Église St. Clothilde, and near the Chamber of Deputies. She had arranged for me to stay with a French family, the Debrayes, in Chantilly, about an hour's train journey out of Paris. It was felt to be much safer to have no contact with Diana. In that way she wouldn't be compromised by being connected, not only with an English girl, but one with false papers.

The family in Chantilly were infinitely kind and felt sorry for the temporarily lonely French-Canadian girl. I had a lovely warm room and, though the strain of keeping up a fictitious past was tricky, I quite enjoyed it. Their daughter, who was about my age, was a delightful companion and we became firm friends, going for long walks in the beautiful forest at Chantilly. No one asked any awkward questions and once again I was grateful for my natural Parisian accent. They firmly believed my story.

Obviously I made some silly mistakes, which were contributory factors towards my eventual arrest. For instance the few letters I wrote, to Daniel and other friends, I signed Antonia. I also wrote to the Spaaks' daughter, whom I had met when she came down to Lancey once, at their Paris address, again signing my own name.

My eighteenth birthday was a day like any other. I couldn't celebrate it as it wasn't the date of birth on my false identity card! Paris was in a fearful state. The Germans were as vicious as cornered rats and knew that it could only be a matter of time. How, when and where would it all end? Ordinary citizens waited, with ice-cold fear in their hearts, for the dreaded knock on the door at dawn, the Gestapo's favourite time for arresting people.

For some time I had been suffering from a grumbling appendix, the pains occasionally being quite acute, so in order to buy a little "safe time", as well as to avoid peritonitis, Diana arranged for me to have it out. This was done at a small hospital near St. Ouen, one of the suburbs of Paris. The nurses were nuns, like those at Quimper so long ago.

I registered as Antoinette Louise Savier. What everyone had forgotten is that when one comes round from an anaesthetic one can say quite unspeakable things; dear old ladies will string four-letter words together, which one would never suspect them of knowing. I chatted away in *English*! Possibly I was swearing, no one told me what I said. Luckily the surgeon and his team were all pro-British, and of course the nuns would never talk anyway, so my secret was safe. The funny sequel to this was when I had my first baby three years after the war. I had to have an anaesthetic and apparently babbled away excitedly in French!

Dear Diana felt it was safe enough to see me in hospital and used to come and visit me every day, which was a great joy and comfort to me. It was a good thing the appendix was removed as it was in a bad state and left a long scar. If only I hadn't been in such pain, I would have enjoyed being looked after, given ice-cream (an unheard-of luxury) and quiet rest in bed. One night there was a familiar sound – bombers. The Citroën factories were at St. Ouen, making military equipment for the Germans. They were the R.A.F.'s target. I lay in bed, helpless, thinking what a rotten end it would be to die in a hospital bed, bombed by my own side! The noise was thunderous and the nuns were tremendously excited. They came into my room and, regardless of their own safety, opened the windows to cheer on the British pilots. It wasn't until a bomb snaked down into a street nearby that they shut the window and left me, saying they would have work to do.

Two days after the operation my side seemed to be on fire. I was also scared stiff. The explosions went on endlessly. The whole night was lit up with searchlights. I held my breath and tears of fear ran down my face. Then I heard the groans and cries of the wounded being brought in by the nuns. There wasn't room for them in the rooms and wards, and they were lying on stretchers and trolleys in the corridors. One, not too badly wounded, was brought in to my room for the night, until room could be found for them all in other hospitals next day. The nuns gave us both a sedative and told me, very quietly, that the raid had been very successful and most of the factory was out of action.

I stayed in for about ten days and, towards the end of September, returned to my lodgings in Chantilly. My stomach was sore but the family were so determined to nurse me back to health that nothing was too much trouble for them. As usual when any illness laid me low, I got boils on my face again. I felt very low, and my convalescence was slow – all energy and hope seemed drained from me.

To cheer me up, the Spaaks asked me over to their flat. I had never met Suzette, Claude's wife, nor seen the flat, so I was most excited. It was fun to meet up with Claude and Ruth again, and we chatted gaily. I never noticed any nervous tension or anxiety. Dutifully, I admired the many Magritte paintings. They were exquisitely painted, but so surrealistic and contrived that I couldn't really appreciate them.

Over tea Claude asked, "You remember the Belgian doctor at St. Pierre de Chartreuse? I've got a chum who needs to go into hiding for a bit. Do you think De Joncker would put him up for a few weeks? In fact, there might be two of them." I presumed that he meant ordinary people like me with false papers, or needing them, and I never hesitated.

"Of course, I'm sure he'd help. What can I do?"

"Well, if you wrote a personal letter to him he'd know these two were genuine, and they would be most grateful."

He dictated a letter which I wrote, merely saying the two were friends of mine, needing shelter and food, and could he please help. I then signed it with my own name: Antonia Lyon-Smith. The name Antoinette Louise Savier would have meant nothing to De Joncker. Later I took the train back out to Chantilly and was so tired by my long day that I went straight to bed.

Madame Debraye was worried by my slow convalescence and insisted on giving me my breakfast in bed. There always seemed to be delicious butter, and nearly real coffee, and occasionally an egg. Like most of the population, in order to exist they had to supplement the very meagre rations with "black market" produce at exorbitant prices.

A couple of days later I went to Paris to see Diana, but in the Rue Casimir Périer I met a very harassed-looking Ruth. I greeted her warmly and couldn't understand the terrified expression on her face and the lowered voice. I could hardly hear her whispered warning, "You must go away – we've got to go into hiding." It was urgent and pleading, and I was utterly puzzled. What *was* she talking about? I tried to ask, "Why? What do you mean? I thought it was your friends who had to go into hiding." But Ruth stopped me and wouldn't say any more, and it was lucky she didn't, for I was genuinely and completely ignorant and in the dark, so could give nothing away later. Ruth kissed me, looking sad and shattered, and we parted. It was the last time we were to meet, but I wasn't to know this and didn't really give much thought to the episode.

At the time I never even asked Claude why I, in particular, should write the letter to De Joncker. It never entered my head. For thirty years I presumed Claude must have been involved on the fringe of the Belgian Resistance in Paris – until I read *The Red Orchestra*. I did vaguely think, after reading it, that there must have been many other well-organized and secret escape routes available to the members of the Trepper organization. The fleeting thought crossed my mind, too, that Claude Spaak, weighing the odds, decided, quite rightly, that the organization was more important than the almost non-existent risk or danger to a girl who could tell the Gestapo nothing in any case. After all, Trepper's girl-friend, Virginia de Winter, might never have been arrested with my telltale letter on her. My naivety and innocence did in fact save my life. What more, you might say, can one ask? Trepper did manage to stay in hiding throughout the rest of the occupation; as did Claude, in a lunatic asylum. Trepper's girl-friend, caught while crossing into the South of France, on her way to De Joncker, spent a hideous winter in prison. One can go on endlessly conjecturing: why hadn't she just memorized the name and address of De Joncker and my name, and destroyed the letter? It is so easy to be "wise after the event". Questioning is pointless – things just happen. Ruth too went into hiding. I never knew where. But Suzette Spaak, who had been organizing an escape route for Jews, was arrested by the Gestapo and sent to Fresnes, where all their prisoners were sent for torture and deportation to concentration camps. She was tortured and shot. The story is told in *The Red*

Orchestra. Nearly everyone who was sent to Fresnes was shot.

After the war Ruth and Claude married, and now live in France. Diana sees them occasionally and I get news of them through her, but have never met them since.

After leaving Ruth in the Rue Casimer Périer, I went back to the house in the Rue du Connétable in Chantilly. I didn't really think that what Ruth had told me affected me personally at all. The boil on my face was very painful and I had to keep putting hot poultices on it. In a day or two it burst, which meant keeping it clean with a bit of Elastoplast over it. As I was housebound, I wrote some letters – one to Daniel, whose home was in Pau, but who was back in Lancey for a spell, and one to Pilar, the Spaaks' daughter, who had given me an address in Belgium to write to. We exchanged girlish confidences from time to time, discussing boyfriends.

I went to bed early on the night of 12th October. My face ached, my period was due and I felt rotten! My mind was a blank, except for feeling sorry for myself. I was good at that!

An electrifying pounding on the door of the Rue du Connétable just before 7 a.m. the next morning woke me with a start. Only the Gestapo would do this. Why? For me? Because of my false French papers? How did they know where I was? How could it possibly concern them? A thousand questions flashed through my barely conscious mind. Fear did all the classical things. My stomach knotted, my mouth became dry and my heart pounded like the beating on the door. My legs turned to water. Madame Debraye went to let them in. What attitude should I adopt? If I dressed hurriedly and seemed frightened I would appear guilty, or so I reasoned to myself. The trembling I couldn't hide, but when they burst into my room without knocking I was putting my dressing gown and slippers on and trying desperately to appear not only unconcerned but astonished and cross that two strange men should dare to come into my bedroom. How could I know, poor foolish creature, that the Gestapo were arresting hundreds of people every day, half of whom at least probably adopted that attitude? They looked the part of the thin-lipped, cruel Gestapo men – slouch felt hats, which they never took off, and belted trenchcoats.

They asked my name and I replied, "Antoinette Louise Savier. Do you want to check my papers? Why have you come so early?" They never answered, and though up till then a tiny sliver of hope made me think it possibly only *was* a genuine checking of papers, their next command shattered any hope, and despair flooded me: "Get dressed quickly. Pack an overnight case. You're coming with us to Headquarters for routine questioning." My mind was racing. I knew no one ever reappeared from Gestapo "routine questioning". I didn't even know what they would be questioning me about. I had no idea what to do or say. They stayed with me while I dressed and questioned me as to my name, insisting that Antoinette Louise Savier was not my real name. All this was done in French through the interpreter, who was with the Gestapo police. I kept denying all knowledge of any other name: "I just don't understand what you want. My name is Antoinette Savier." I went on repeating this, playing for time and worried about the Debrayes. What would happen to them? They had taken me in in all good faith, believing me to be a French-Canadian girl. This might get them into awful trouble and they knew nothing of the deception played on them. I hated the thought of the kind parents and their friendly daughter suffering on my behalf. But what could I *do*? I was determined to go on asserting my French name. It was the only thought I could cling to for the time being. I must appear nonchalant and unconcerned and stop the Debrayes worrying too.

"What about breakfast?" I asked.

"No time. You are coming with us now, for interrogation."

That word fell like lead on my ears, but I felt I mustn't show it. The Debrayes were told to get into the car too. I did my best to reassure them – it was all a terrible mistake; they would soon be home. Feeling like a heroine in a novel, I asked if I might have an apple to chew in the car, in lieu of breakfast. Each mouthful stuck in my throat, but I was determined to finish it, and even tried to chat unconcernedly on the drive to Paris. "What a treat to drive in a car. It's ages since I've been in one." My mind raced. Could I escape if the car had to stop? Obviously not. The Debrayes would pay for it. And I wouldn't get far with nowhere to go. Where were they taking me? I knew Paris well. If it were any ordinary German police headquarters all might still be explained away, my papers examined and myself released. With terror I watched, as in some inevitable nightmare, the official car sweep into the Rue des Saussaies. This was the main Gestapo headquarters in Paris. No one stayed there. Most were sent to Fresnes, the dreaded prison, and most, if not all, were shot after unspeakable torture had made death itself a merciful end.

Here I was, separated from the Debrayes – whom I never saw again. I learned long afterwards that they were sent home that day. It was lucky for them that they knew nothing and that I had resisted the temptation to gain prestige by confiding to the daughter that I was in fact English, with false French papers. On and off, throughout that long day, I kept telling the Gestapo "Chief" that the Debrayes knew nothing.

I was taken to Room 333 – a number indelibly printed on my mind. It was a large room with a big desk, a sofa, comfy chairs and a tubby pink-faced little man behind the desk. His name was Müller. His eyes were of steel and his voice rasped the questions, duly repeated by an interpreter in French. Also in the room were at least two other Gestapo officials and a blonde secretary. I was made to stand while questions about my identity were shouted at me. For nearly two hours I continued the charade of Antoinette Louise Savier, and then one of the men shoved a book under my eyes.

"Then, who is this Antonia Lyon-Smith?"

There were all my school books, various letters and so on, all bearing my own name. It must have seemed so crassly amateur. Of course they already knew the answers to all the questions, but I didn't know that at the time. I shrugged my shoulders and accepted the inevitable. It was a relief to be myself and be English again. They brought in another interpreter and continued the interrogation in English. For a while I relaxed. They only seemed to want to know my life history. I knew nothing could happen to my parents and, for good measure, when they asked me about my father, I proudly promoted him to General (though the last time I had seen him nearly four years ago he had only been a Colonel. I wasn't far out; he was in fact a Brigadier-General!) and said with a flickering show of spirit,

"Yes, and he's in the Royal Horse Artillery and jolly well winning the war." There was a faint show of interest among the men in the room: "*Sein Vater ein General.*" Obviously they had a healthy respect for senior-ranking military officers. However, they had none for the daughter.

On and on went the questioning. Who were my grandparents? What were their names? Once again the name of Hellmuth had an ominous ring. Still, my mother *was* Canadian, and my father and his ancestors completely British; so I didn't have to worry on that score. What did they want me for? Now that they knew I was English, surely they would send me to join Nanny.

I was tired and, strangely enough, hungry. The interrogation, all the while standing up, had taken all the morning with only the apple in the car to keep me going. I badly wanted to go to the lavatory and asked if I could. My German wasn't very good, but I could understand a few words here and there. They were sending for another woman, a guard, in order to search me before escorting me to the lavatory. The woman was a brutish, fat and ugly creature who made me strip and handled me roughly. She searched my hair, my anus and vagina. It was a miserable and mortifying experience. I had no idea what they were looking for. (Of course years later, when I had read stories of Resistance and British Intelligence officers parachuted into France, I realized they had been searching for the lethal cyanide pill agents were provided with and which they took if they had the slightest opportunity, before torture forced them to reveal any information.)

They brought me sandwiches and I was allowed to sit down before the interrogation began again. My brain was already reeling from the four solid hours in the morning. I hadn't been able to wash or even comb my hair, and my boil was throbbing under its dressing. Fear, mingled with abject sorrow, brought me close to tears.

The really serious part of the questioning began now. I could tell that the German interpreter, who spoke very good English, was fairly sure there was nothing more to my story, but the other interrogator obviously loathed me. On and on they probed. Why had my mother and I come over to France in the first place? Who had we stayed with? I felt it was safe to mention Diana, who was, after all, French by marriage. (Again, it wasn't until afterwards that I learned they took Diana in to the Gestapo Headquarters that night for questioning, before releasing her the next day. Neither I nor the Gestapo, luckily, knew that Diana's flat in Paris was one of the places which Yeo Thomas, the "White Rabbit", a man of indescribable bravery, used as a meeting place.)

They then started to ask about my false papers. I said some friends had got them for me, but I didn't know who'd made them. It was about this time, to stop myself from thinking about what might happen to me, that I concentrated on the desk. On it, to my horror, appeared to be a thumb screw. I felt physically sick at the sight, wondering when they would use it. Of course it was only a machine for punching holes in paper, but I'd never seen one of those either and, in the frenzied state my mind was in, all the horrifying stories of the Gestapo came back to me.

Suddenly the Chief, the pink-faced short man, began to lose his temper at my repeated ignorance of everything. He screamed at me and banged the desk, leaping to his feet. I was afraid he would come round and start hitting me. What should I say or do? The questions were shouted at me again and again in a confused jumble: "Who procured your identity card?" "A friend." By now I realized that the Spaaks must be in the Resistance and that maybe their friends had been picked up with my letter on them. I must protect Ruth at all costs. She was, as far as I knew, in Paris. The pink-faced man screamed in fury, "Where are they? You know it is through them we have found you." I remembered my letter to the Spaak daughter. Somewhere among my papers there had been a reply, saying they were leaving Paris. At the time I hadn't attached any importance to it. Maybe the letters had been intercepted. In all innocence I said. "They must be in Belgium somewhere – I don't know where." The second German, who was assisting the interpreter, started going purple with fury. He kept saying "*Sie muss erschossen werden.*" "*Sie muss nach Fresnes gehen.*" (She must be shot. She must go to Fresnes.) The interpreter kept trying to calm him. He obviously wanted to help me and could tell I was a completely useless, helpless pawn. The strain of the long day began to take its toll. I could hardly keep awake. Dusk was falling. Where would I go? What would they do to me? I understood the oft-repeated phrase of the fanatical Nazi who wanted me to be shot. I was allowed to sit, but they kept on at me, shining a bright light and, whenever my head fell forward in sleep, shaking my arm to wake me.

"We know who you wrote to? Did he get the false identity card? Did he? Did he?" I fell into that particular trap and vehemently denied that it was Durand. "So you *did* write to someone near Grenoble?" I was incapable of understanding the devious trickery of their questioning I had had no training, no experience whatsover. They mentioned Lancey and my "so-called friends" there.

I was in pain by now and my barely-healed appendix scar throbbed. I could feel that my period had started and I had nothing with me. The pain in my stomach made me bend double. If only I could sleep. Different Gestapo officials came and went, but the interpreter stayed, and I sensed increasingly that he was protecting me. I longed for a hot drink. It was now past nine o'clock. Eventually, more asleep than awake, I heard myself say "Durand". They scorned this first of all by saying everyone was called Durand; it is a name like Smith. Then, using the same method of denying and justifying, they told me it was Durand who had given them my address anyway. I was long past understanding what I was supposed to have said or done, or anyone else, and utter weariness overcame me. I fell over the table fast asleep.

I don't know for how long I slept, but when I woke up the "Chief" had gone; only the interpreter and secretary were left with me. When I realized that it wasn't just a nightmare, but that it was dark and I was still in the office of Zimmer 333 I couldn't help crying. I had to ask for some sanitary towels and the secretary, who was a kind woman, went and got me a packet. She also gave me a cup of coffee and some cheese. Then the door burst open and there was the power-crazy Nazi shouting abuse at the interpreter and secretary. Pointing a finger trembling with fury at me, he told them to have me driven to Fresnes straight away. It was late and they must hurry. It certainly was late. A hurried discussion took place as to what should happen to me. Quietly but firmly, the interpreter, Karl Gagel, won the argument and insisted that I was not fit enough to go to Fresnes that night and could spend the night in one of the cells in the cellars of the Rue des Saussaies.

Karl tried to comfort me, talking reassuringly. Gradually I pulled myself together. I had been lucky that day – no torture, only the bright light in my face and being kept awake. Later, about 10 p.m., I heard the most terrifying and hellish sound I had ever heard. It was a long way off. It was a man screaming, yelling in long-drawn-out, agonizing screams, tortured to breaking point. I could feel myself going white with shock and fear. Karl Gagel did his best to talk loudly to drown it, but it persisted until a sudden silence presumably meant that he had fainted. I looked wildly about me. I would prefer to be shot than tortured. I questioned the interpreter, "How long will they keep me here? When can I go? I know nothing." He could give no answer. "Come. I'll take you to a cell for tonight. Tomorrow we will see." While his back was turned, feeling very daring, I tore the page off the diary on the desk, 13th October, and kept it as a reminder.

Down long winding stairs we clattered, past armed sentries on guard duty. Just below ground level, where the safes must have been kept in the old days, was a solid iron grille, with a barred locked door. This led down a concrete corridor, damp and cold, to a second locked door. The keys clanked and echoed in the bare passage which ended in another room, behind bars. It wasn't a room – it was a bare concrete vault, filthy and stinking. Off this room was yet another locked door leading into the second cell. This was where I was locked in. The only thing in it was an old iron bedstead with a filthy damp straw mattress on it. Otherwise it was bare, empty except for dirt. The small frosted window was high up and barred. It was in these cells that prisoners were kept between interrogations. Sheer panic overcame me. "What happens if I want to go to the lavatory?" Karl Gagel explained, "There is a bell there. A guard will come for you, but don't ring it between 8 p.m. and 8 a.m." My heart sank still further; gastroenteritis was no respecter of the clock. I didn't know how long I would be kept there; despair and fear filled my mind. The interpreter said he would see me next day and left, locking the door behind him and then the three other doors, which I could hear clicking and clanking, getting gradually fainter until, I could hear no more.

My self-control went completely. I cried as though I were a child – loudly, noisily, the tears streaming down my face. I shouted, "I don't want to die – I want Mummy." I was ashamed of my outburst but was incapable of stopping. Huge sobs shook me. Then a strange, miraculous thing happened. I found myself on my knees, praying fervently to God. For the last year or more I had been an avowed atheist. Now, with a pure unpremeditated instinct, I was praying, praying for comfort, for strength, for love, for help. Instinct was stronger than any reasoning. For ages I talked out loud through my tears. I had no handkerchief; there was nothing to mop up the streaming tears. I begged God to forgive me. "How *could* I have not believed in You, if the first time I'm in trouble, the first thing I do is to pray to You. You don't mind, do You? I expect its happened to other people too." I cried and prayed for ages before utter exhaustion made me lie down, in my coat, on the greasy, blood-stained straw mattress and fall asleep. I didn't sleep for long. A sudden familiar pain tore through my bowels. The gastro-enteritis attacks came at intervals; sometimes there were days between them, sometimes weeks. They usually passed in about two hours, during which time I would feel faint and sweat with pain. I had no watch, but the dim light told me that dawn was only just breaking. I couldn't ring for a guard; the only alternative was to foul my cell and this I was determined not to do. I lay as still as possible, shivering with cold, and clenching every muscle in my body. I wondered how long I could endure the pain and lost count of time. All my concentration was needed to control my body. If I had known there were to be five months of this I would probably have gone out of my mind. The blessed relief of not seeing into the future is not properly appreciated.

My ears strained for a sound and at last came the rattling and clanking of the big bunch of keys, opening the four doors. It was the blond, tough secretary, who, albeit with bad grace, nevertheless volunteered to take me to the washroom and lavatory before starting work. I realized quite soon that I owed my life to the interpreter and the secretary, but I couldn't envisage the complicated ensuing emotional tangle. I was a long time in the lavatory and the poor secretary kept telling me to hurry up or she would be in trouble. When I saw my appearance in the mirror I was horrified. I had not been able to wash or comb my hair for twenty-four hours. I did what I could without a comb, and washed my face and hands. My hair needed washing badly, but I had felt too ill to do it before my arrest. Back down to my cell we went and I was told I would be interrogated again. Once I was left on my own, self-pity and fear overwhelmed me. There was no one to see me or hear me cry.

Karl Gagel came for me later on and brought me a cup of coffee. I dreaded going back to room 333. I had cause to. The half-crazy fanatical Nazi was in the room. He exploded with fury when he saw me, obviously shouting words to the effect that I was wasting their time: I should be disposed of, shot. More questions and answers, more or less the same as on the previous day. They wanted details of the past four years – how I had spent them, and where, and with whom. They were determined to prove that I was part of some Résistance organization. I half wished I *had* been doing something useful, to make my arrest more valid, something more exciting than just writing a letter. Then it was back down to my barred cell. For a week I was convinced I would be shot. For a week I wanted desperately to live – to see my parents again, to see England, to know

England had won the war. I spent most of the time crying and praying. I hardly dared to ring the bell for the guard to take me to the lavatory. They were all surly louts who looked on any prisoner as scum, pushing me along with the butts of their rifles: "*Schnell, schnell*" or "*Raus, raus*", whichever was appropriate.

One day I was lying asleep on the dirty bed – there was nothing else to do. There was no chair, no table, no book, nothing – when I was woken up by the jangling of keys. "Not another interrogation," I hoped, but whoever it was stopped at the cell outside mine. I heard footsteps, a scuffle, the thud of a body, then more footsteps and the doors locking. My heart beat fast. There must be another prisoner there. I lay very still. Eventually a heart-rending sound reached me. It was a man, crying, just as I had cried. I longed to comfort him, but the door was locked between us. Should I call to him, try to talk to him? With sudden perception and pity, I knew how humiliated he would be. He thought he was alone, that no one could witness his unhappiness. So I kept as quiet as possible; he mustn't know I was next door. They came for him later and he never came back.

It was cold and damp in the cell. My meals were brought by a guard, and after eating them I would stop shivering for an hour or so while a faint warmth enabled me to go to sleep.

The days passed, so alike in misery, cold and dirt that they merged into one another. I still cried, but less now because I was very tired. Why they kept me there I never knew. Did they hope that at some stage I might remember a vital bit of information, or was it purely Karl's influence?

Often at night I wrestled with my chronic complaint, rolling on the straw mattress, sweat from the acute pains pouring off my body. It was not a very subtle form of torture. I knew I must smell awful. The clothes I was wearing when I was arrested were all I had, and they hadn't been washed or changed for over two weeks. Every morning the same secretary took me up to let me wash my face and hands. I wondered if I dared ask whether I might wash my hair one morning. Karl Gagel saw me every day, either at an interrogation or sometimes to bring me a meal. I realized that he was becoming fond of me, but I couldn't imagine why. I must have looked terrible, and my pathetic behaviour seemed more likely to arouse contempt than sympathy. However, such strange things do happen and I was certainly extremely grateful to him. The hours I spent on my own made me long to talk to anyone I saw. Solitary confinement is hard to bear.

It was a strict rule that the door between the two cells be kept locked, even if there was no one in the other cell. Sometimes the guards were lax about this, and usually I let it go. Three locked doors were plenty to keep me in! One night, after I had been there about three weeks, when the guard brought me back from my last visit to the lavatory at 8 p.m., for some unaccountable reason I asked him to be sure to lock it. I lay down and drifted into a sort of semi-sleep when suddenly I heard a loud commotion of clattering feet, clanking keys and fierce shouting. My heart bled for what I supposed to be another young Resistance worker defying his jailers. He was flung into the cell, as I had heard others pushed, and left. For a while there was silence, then a drunken, furious pounding at the outer cell door, accompanied by the shaking of the bars of the grille, made me curiously afraid. Prisoners never had the strength to act so violently after hours of interrogation and torture. What did it mean? Then, with horror, as he started to yell abuse, in *German*, I recognized the voice of the fanatical Nazi Gestapo official who had been present through nearly all my interrogations. What on earth was he doing *in a cell*? He certainly sounded drunk, but surely they wouldn't have put him in one of their own cells because of that? I had no time to think further. He obviously became aware of the fact that he was in the next cell to "Fraulein Schmidt", as he called me. He turned his attention to the door between the cells and tried to open it. His fury knew no bounds when he found it was locked. He yelled, *"Fraulein Schmidt, sie sind da?"* and pounded wildly on the door. He shouted obscene things, most of which I could not understand, but I understood very clearly that when he had broken down the door he intended to kill me. He kicked the door, he tried to wrench the handle off; the door shook. I lay there trembling with fear, thanking God I had made the guard lock it. What if it didn't hold? I knew he would do the most dreadful things to me before he killed me, in order to get his revenge for my not having been sent to Fresnes or shot. He kept it up for about an hour and, though it was the middle of the night, my fear was such that I rang the bell for the guard. As he approached I called to him in my school-girl German, unable to control the shaking of my voice. "Please stop him; he is trying to break down the door; he wants to kill me." I heard, in dazed relief, the reprimand, and gathered he had been severely warned. For a while he went on muttering to himself, then must have thrown himself on the bed and fallen into a drunken stupor. I was in such a state of shock I could only lie there rigid, wondering if he would try again and how long the door would hold. He was a very big man.

I heard them come for him next morning and lead him away. When the secretary came for me, I asked her what had happened. Apparently, during a drunken brawl he had shot and killed one of his fellow Gestapo officials. It had happened in the building and they had nowhere else to put him for the night. He would be tried and sent to prison. I only understood fragments of the story. Later I asked Karl Gagel, who told me in English, and who was appalled when I told him of the terrifying night I had had.

In a way, after he had gone, I began to feel hopeful that perhaps I mightn't be shot after all. He had obviously been mad in his obsessive hatred for me.

Another carbuncle appeared, this time in the middle of my back. I could only lie on my side and it was very painful. Diana had brought a sleeping bag to the Rue des Saussaies for me, and a change of clothes and some underwear. So I could at least keep warm with all my clothes on inside the sleeping bag. It was still only November, not yet desperately cold.

The lump on my back grew and gave me a fever. Being right on my spine I couldn't get at it and I implored the secretary to ask if I could see a doctor. Gruffly I was told that there was no doctor in the building. I lay in a stupor, the fever making me sleepy, the pain waking me fitfully. Finally Karl interceded on my behalf and volunteered to walk me to a German hospital in Paris. I had to show my back to the "Chief" to prove I wasn't pretending. It was a long walk, over a mile, and I felt I would never make it. At the military hospital there was little sympathy for a prisoner of the Gestapo. All the overworked doctor could do to burst the carbuncle was to offer to put a *ventouse* over it. Karl explained what this medieval process involved. A heated glass cup would be slapped on my back to draw the poison out. I was scared stiff, but there was no alternative. It all took place in a large so-called surgery, full of soldiers and nurses. I stripped my top half and lay on my tummy, gritting my teeth. Karl gave me his hand to hold and I wondered even then, through the haze of pain, whether he was not becoming too fond of me. It hurt abominably, being just over the spine, with little flesh to protect it. It burst through many holes into the *venthouse*. I clenched his hand and bit my lip, but made no sound. I could do that later in the privacy of my cell, but not in front of Germans.

Initially there was some relief and I thought it would get better. Karl held my arm to support me on the way back. I thanked him with real warmth for his kindness and was amazed to realize that, even in the Gestapo, there were good and kind people. How, then, could they work for the Gestapo?

The interrogations became more spaced out. Occasionally in the corridors I would be marched past another prisoner going for interrogation – harrowing sights: broken arms hanging limp, faces purple and swollen from beatings. Once, during an air-raid, when all prisoners were taken down into the air-raid shelters, I saw that wonderful Irish priest, Father O'Hara, who had been so kind and helpful to everyone in the barracks in Grenoble. He looked straight past me, deliberately not recognizing me for safety's sake, and I did the same. I was learning.

Now, when I did go up to Room 333, they would harangue me about the war. I knew that the British, helped by America and Russia, were slowly and definitely winning the war, but obviously couldn't begin to guess how it would eventually be brought about. I was full of praise for the Russians. They were our allies at the time, and I was ignorant of Russian politics and behaviour as I had been of the Germans. Stupidly I would say,

"We will win the war. I *know* it, and then you'll be sorry." But they only laughed at me,

"Oh no, we won't. We'll be laughing at you having problems with Russia. We'll have the last laugh!" I couldn't understand what they meant, but how true in retrospect!

After a week or so – it was impossible to keep track of dates – my back started to suppurate badly, which was not surprising as I slept in my clothes and could never wash properly. My clothes and sleeping bag began to stink of the pus. The fever came back and Karl began to worry again. The pain wasn't as bad, but the wound was just going rotten, with no clean dressing since it had been operated on. Once again I had to show it to the "Chief", who held a handkercheif to his nose and agreed I should see a French doctor. The Germans had no time for a useless prisoner. A French doctor was found, just in time, as the flesh had rotted to the bare bone and nitrate of silver had to be applied. Naturally no penicillin or anti-biotics were available. I was given the precious little stick and told to rub it on the wound every day. Karl did it for me as I couldn't reach. He was very gentle and I talked to him, asking him where and when he had learned his excellent English. He told me that he had lived in England for years, studying and learning the language. Slowly my back got better.

Now I wasn't quite so lonely in my cell at night; a rat woke me up one night, eating an apple core I had thrown away after my supper. I was delighted to see him and after that used to throw down the odd crust deliberately to entice him out. I tried to keep awake so as not to miss him, but I didn't see him very often. I seemed to sleep a lot.

About the middle of November, after I had been in the Rue des Saussaies for perhaps six weeks, Karl Gagel announced a splendid surprise,

"Your cousin wants to see how you are. She is coming this afternoon with the medicines you need and some clean underwear. You can have tea in the little room off the office of room 333. The secretary, Lisa, will stay with you." It was unbelievable. Surely it must have been the first time in the history of the Gestapo that this had happened. I was overwhelmed at the thought of seeing Diana and actually talking to someone who wasn't in the Gestapo.

It was an incongruous reunion. We hugged each other with emotion and it was hard to know what to talk about first. We obviously had to be guarded in what we said. The young secretary didn't speak much English, or French, but Diana was afraid of hidden microphones. Nowadays any eighteen-year-old, having been brought up on "bugging" on television, would think of it, but I didn't even know such a device existed!

Tea was brought in on a tray and *bread and butter* – unheard of luxuries. I couldn't conceal my hunger and greedily ate the lot. (My ability, when fit, always to eat whatever was put in front of me, and to sleep soundly, must be the reason why I survived that nightmare existence and was able to lead a normal life – and be normal – after it all.)

After the initial visit Diana was allowed to visit me about once a fortnight, which gave me something to look forward to. I asked her to bring me some books, as the long hours with nothing to do except sit and listen for the keys in the four locked doors were cruel. I never knew by whom, or how, Diana's visits were arranged.

My back healed very slowly. Only once did I steel myself to reach back and touch the bare bone of the spine before the healthy flesh started to cover it. The scar it still there.

Those five months are impossible to write about dispassionately, and yet there were times, when I first realized that Karl Gagel was falling in love with me, or when, from the sheer relief of not being shot, or being sent to Fresnes, or being perpetually in pain, or crying, that I was content to let each day happen. It all had an unreal feeling; one day it would be over but in the meantime I was alive. It is difficult to put across that emotion to people who have not lived for a week in the certain knowledge that it is their last.

Karl Gagel not only did what he could to be kind, he looked at me with compassion, and indeed with love. I didn't know what to do about it. My deep gratitude for all I owed him turned into fondness too. I looked forward to seeing him, and soon I was seeing him ever more often. This was because of my visits to Doctor Raiga.

My whole system had become infected by the festering carbuncle and staphylococci were rampant in my body. Suppurating sores broke out all over my body. They went bad and had to be treated. So, the long walks to see Doctor Raiga took place every two days. He scraped off the scabs, dusted some disinfectant powder on them, and put little dressings on each one.

It was during one of these walks that Karl confessed,

"Tonia, I don't know what to do. What is happening to me? It is a shameful thing for me but I can't help it. I love you." The psychological and emotional problems that this would present in the future months I could not foresee. I lived from day to day; all constructive reasoning had been replaced by the will to live through this present hell, to live to see my own country, my parents. It must end one day. The future would look after itself.

I looked at him searchingly,

"Why, and how can you possibly love me? For one thing I must look a mess."

"No. To me you are beautiful. You are uncomplicated and honest and, despite what you've been through, dignified." If he had seen or heard my uncontrolled crying and shouts of despair, he might have thought differently. I was starved of affection and felt utterly lost. I owed my life to him and, with my naturally affectionate nature, I trusted him and thought I loved him too. He kissed me. We were on our way back from Doctor Raiga and it was in the Tuileries Gardens. There was nothing unusual in France about a young man and a girl kissing each other in public, but I wondered what on earth they would say if they knew that one was a Gestapo interpreter and the other an English prisoner. It was a situation fraught with guilt, shame, gratitude, and, in those early days, of love.

Christmas was only a week or so away. What a miserable way to spend it. The cell became so cold, half-basement as it was, and the breath froze on my lips. Though most of my days were spent lying down, as there was no chair, I always felt tired, and thought it must be the long walks to have my sores dressed every two days.

I learned from Karl that Berlin and other German cities were being heavily bombed, and the little secretary's family in Berlin had been bombed. It made no difference to her attitude to me and she still took me up to the washroom every morning. Apart from the morning cup of "coffee", I had two meals, one at midday, consisting of a bowl of sauerkraut or some vegetable stew, and in the evening either cold sausage or cheese. Not very much, but enough to warm me for a short while. The cold was utterly penetrating and stopped all thought. Even the rat gave up coming out.

Just before Christmas the secretary did the kindest possible thing. She volunteered to give up her Christmas day in order to take me to my cousin's flat in the Rue Casimir Périer. It was unbelievable. This was a truly Christian gesture.

She walked with me to the flat, and Diana and I hugged each other very tight. It was an awkward and embarrassing day for everyone. Micky, my cousin's daughter, was there, which helped a lot, as she was only twelve or so. The meal must have been delicious but it was difficult to know what to say. One had to be so guarded and concentration was impossible. It must have been just as awkward for the secretary, too. She daren't leave my side. My one idea was to telephone Daniel Héry and find out if he was all right. I was still very fond of him. I tried to telephone when I went to the lavatory, but Diana intercepted me and gently and quietly broke it to me that Daniel had also been arrested, but it was hoped that his release might be negotiated, as his only crime had been knowing me. I was horrified to learn of this. When the Hotel at Lancey was searched, because of my being traced there through the fatal letter to Doctor De Joncker, Daniel and Durand both had letters from me in their rooms and these had been found. Durand was sent to a concentration camp for a very long time. I had no address with which to get in touch with him, so I never knew when he got back, and never heard from him. Diana and I couldn't talk, so she played the piano and we tried to sing tunes from the 'thirties. Our voices choked with tears, thinking of the happy times when we had sung those same songs in Concarneau, so many years ago.

I dreaded going back to my dark and freezing cell. I clung to Diana and could hardly bear to leave. I felt like a child from whom all security has been snatched. It had been a glorious but painful interlude, upsetting Diana as much as me.

Day followed freezing day in a jumble of pain, both in my stomach from the repeated attacks of gastro-enteritis and from my infected sores. Mentally, too, a jumble of emotions racked me – the impassioned love-making of Karl whenever he came to the cell, and the knowledge that I shouldn't enjoy kissing him. He never, I'm afraid – for no true story is worth its salt without a rape – tried to seduce me. He knew I was a virgin. Looking back, it seemed incredible that it was automatically accepted and respected, by French and German alike.

Every now and then I would be taken up to Room 333 for a routine interrogation. I think that at last they were beginning to realize that I really *did* know nothing. My things had all been forwarded from the Rue du Connetable in Chantilly and were either at my cousin's flat or in some dark cupboard. I plucked up courage to ask if I might have my teddy bear, at least, as some sort of comfort. I could have wept when I was told he had been ripped apart, searched for secret messages. What a heroic, glorious end for a teddy bear! No other can have suffered such a fate.

Then doctor Raiga decided to experiment on me. The sores were getting no better. In fact they were spreading, and the boils were returning. He tried taking half a pint of blood from the vein in my arm and injecting it into my bottom. It was quite painful and took rather a long time, but the idea was on the same principle as a smallpox inoculation. He did this about once a week, and during the long walks to and from the surgery Karl would make plans for our future. He lived in Worms and wanted me to marry him. I tried to demur, but in my weakened state found it difficult to reason with him. I explained that I would have to talk to my parents first.

123

At about this time Karl started to bring pressure to bear on me. At first it was the fact that he loved me so desperately that he found it impossible to do his work properly unless I agreed to marry him. This implied that if he didn't carry out his duties efficiently he might be transferred to another Gestapo headquarters. Obviously if this happened and there was no one to look after me, I would go straight to Fresnes. None of this was said outright, merely inferred. So, shamefully and with the knowledge that I was too ill to survive Fresnes, I went along with his plans and even accepted a ring from him. It was a beautiful black pearl and must have cost him a fortune. I thought of Peter Dougall in the *Caserne* at St. Denis. What would he think of my behaviour? Poor Karl, his happiness when I put the ring on touched me deeply. Why did these complications have to test my worn-out state beyond endurance? I had done nothing – but nothing – to arouse any feelings of love. Pity, perhaps, unconsciously, but not love.

The end of January was sheer torture. The cold invaded every bone in my body. The walks to the doctor did not warm me because I could only walk slowly. The doctor was now taking pus from one boil and injecting it into another – a refinement on his blood transfusion experiments and infinitely more painful. It was clear that I had septicaemia. In my weakened state I cried each time these experiments were carried out. He meant well probably, but still it was torture.

One person who visited the "Chief" in room 333 was John Amery. He was the son of Leo Amery, who, I think, was Secretary of State for India during the war, and brother of Julian Amery. He was the last traitor to be executed at the Tower. He asked to see me. All I knew was that he was English. (I had never heard of his father.) I could not believe that of his own free will (he *appeared* to be a free agent) any English person could possibly be on friendly terms with the Gestapo and actually collaborating with them. I was shocked to hear him praise the Germans – their efficiency and powers of organization. He told me of his attractive French wife and tried to convince me that the Germans were not so bad after all.

"Do you realize," he said, "when the Germans win the war, we will have the Duke of Windsor as King of occupied England. He is a great admirer of the Germans and of Germany. The Germans will treat England well if he is King." To me this was sheer raving lunacy. For a man like that even to talk of a member of the Royal Family shattered me. I got up, too frightened to say more than, "I do not want to listen to you any more. The Germans won't win anything. Please can I go back to my cell?" I have no idea why I was made to meet him. To my surprise I wasn't punished for behaving so rudely. Apparently the Germans all despised him.

Karl asked me if I would like to see *Die Fledermaus*. I have already indicated how abysmally ignorant I was. To demonstrate this still further, I have to admit that I had never heard of *Die Fledermaus*. I was ashamed to confess my ignorance to a German. But I felt, as it turned out, quite rightly, that this was something I would never see or hear again. It was being performed by the Berlin Operatic Society and the Berlin Philharmonic Orchestra. It would make a wonderful change from the endless black nights in my cell.

It was an extraordinary sensation. The Palais de Chaillot, a modern Opera House in the Champs de Mars, was fully packed with Germans. There were many women in uniform *"souris"* (mice) as they were called. They were the equivalent of the A.T.S. and W.A.A.F. What struck me very forcibly was the ugliness and age of the hundreds, if not thousands, of uniformed Germans. I thought back to the Storm Troopers in Concarneau – tall, blond and young – and even the state of the troops in Paris when I had spent the year in Neuilly. These were pale scrapings of the barrel, and I felt a leap of hope. Naturally it was a strange feeling to be aware that I was not only the only foreigner present, but English at that. Of course I should not have gone, but I was determined to enjoy the performance. It was unbelievably beautiful. I drowned in the music. Nowadays one's ears are deadened by endless music of every description, from "pop" to classical. But I had heard no music for months, years even. The performance entranced me. Tears of joy, for a change, poured down my cheeks, until the tiredness and emotion overcame me and I fell fast asleep! What a waste!

By the middle of February I couldn't manage to walk to the doctor very often. What was worse, I couldn't keep up the pretence of affection towards Karl. I dreaded his presence, longing only for sleep and warmth.

He began to use a form of blackmail. Fairly subtly at first:

"Your cousin, Madame Provost, might know more than you. Perhaps we ought to have her in for questioning." My heart missed a beat. I loved my cousin and couldn't bear the thought of her being arrested. I knew that this was a favourite method of the Gestapo – threatening the families of prisoners, in order to make them give away secrets or names of other agents. As I knew nothing of Diana's activities I couldn't even be grateful for that fact – but in retrospect . . . I was determined to prevent this, and pretended all was well between Karl and me.

The septicaemia worsened, which was hardly surprising in such filthy conditions. The last month of my time in solitary confinement merged in a blur of fever, pain and delirium. Odd incidents stood out. One of them was another very surprising visitor – P. G. Wodehouse. He lived in Paris during the war, and was later forgiven for having done so freely. It was kind of him to come and see me, but nevertheless, it was a shock to me. He tried to comfort me, sitting on the edge of my iron bedstead, where I lay hot with fever.

"The Germans aren't so bad, are they? They might have sent you to Fresnes."

I tried to sort out in my befuddled mind how he could have known I was in the Rue des Saussaies. Who did he know in the Gestapo? I had really nothing to say to him, and felt too ill to make an effort. My eyes closed. He must have thought I was asleep and he left. To this day I don't know how he found out where I was or why he came to see me.

February dragged into March. How long was this mental and physical torture going on for? Abscesses now started in my ears and still there were no medicines for me to take, either for the enteritis or the earache. Each night was a long, black, freezing hell of pain. When I was exhausted from crying, I would sleep till the pain woke me again. Though the walk to the doctor meant fresh air and exercise, it drained me both mentally and physically, as I had to reason with Karl on the way there and back. I became an automaton, barely alive or aware.

Doctor Raiga, always keen on experimental work, wanted to try lancing the abscess in the ear with a syringe, and transfer it to another boil on my body – which was completely covered in sores by this time. My self-control snapped. For months I had submitted to extremely painful treatment, but the agony in my ears was so acute it was driving me mad. I knew if he did that, I *would* go mad. I screamed, lying there in the surgery, and Karl rushed in from the waiting room. I flung myself at him, sobbing and moaning, my head in my hands as I tried in vain to ease the pain. Between my cries, I told Karl,

"I can't stand it. He wants to put a needle in my inner ear, without anaesthetic. Please don't let him! Take me away! I never want to come back! I can't bear it!" I was hysterical. Karl led me away, staggering, my balance affected by the roaring of pus-filled ears, and put me in a car to drive me back to the Gestapo.

I don't remember the next few days. I was semi-conscious and seriously ill. Possibly the Gestapo thought I might die on their hands – an innocent English girl and the daughter of a General. It was 13th March, 1944, and they may have been worried about possible repercussions. Anyway Karl arranged for me to go to my cousin's flat in the Rue Casimir Périer. I would be under house arrest, in other words not allowed out unless Karl took me. I was driven to the flat – in excruciating pain.

No words can adequately describe what it felt like to arrive at the flat. I fell into Diana's arms and she carried me to her daughter's bed. To be in a soft bed with pillows and sheets, to be warm – it felt like going straight to Heaven – if it hadn't been for the searing pain in my ears. Even though it was evening Diana got her own doctor, who immediately gave me morphine, knowing that much more of the sort of agony I had been enduring for weeks might well have unhinged my mind completely. It was the most glorious sensation. All pain ceased and I seemed to float, suspended on a cloud in the middle of nowhere. For days, perhaps weeeks, I lay in bed, under sedation, with kind and gentle treatment. It was sheer joy to be able to walk from one room to another, to be able to go to the lavatory on my own when I wanted. To have hot drinks and all the nourishing foods, like arrowroot, that Diana could get for me. Rationing didn't really work; there wasn't enough to go round anyway. There was no milk or butter, even for children. Everything had to be obtained through the black market.

VIII
❧ Finale ❧

WHILE I WAS recovering Karl left me alone, and, being young, I was soon fit again. Diana's care, the cleanliness, warmth and rest brought back my strength. Diana's doctor managed to produce some medicines of sorts, and even the septicaemia slowly healed. There was only one bedroom in the flat, apart from Diana's, so when Micky came home for the holidays, it was decided that it wouldn't be breaking the house-arrest rule too badly if I slept next door.

Madame Caldagues lived in the flat next door and was an old friend. She was a charming, vague and motherly person who made me very welcome and comfortable. She prepared a little bedroom for me, and each night I would slip next door, getting back in time for breakfast in the morning. Madame Caldagues had a very nice son of seventeen called Michel.

In April, when I was better, Karl rang up Diana to say he would come and take me out for exercise. When I heard this I was terrified. I had to tell Diana my predicament.

"What *shall* I do? He saved my life. He's in love with me and wants to marry me; but I can't bear the thought of seeing him again even though I am really grateful to him." Diana was worried and upset. We were at his mercy and we knew it. She advised me as best she could:

"Be grateful to him but try and get out of this

entanglement; delay it till after the war; it must end soon."

It was a lovely spring day when Karl collected me. No doctor to go to, just a walk through Paris. To me the heartbreaking beauty of it conflicted with the twisted agony of my mind. How was I going to deal with this problem? His joy at seeing me again was sincere and unfeigned:

"You were beautiful in prison, but now I fall in love all over again. You are so very lovely."

We sat on a bench in the Tuileries, and I said,

"You know, Karl, it will be so difficult for us. What will our families think if we don't tell them first?"

At once he became hysterical, walking away, his arms beating the air wildly.

"I can't bear the thought of losing you. You *must* be my wife. I've been so patient. You *and* your cousin will come back to the Rue des Saussaies if this is how you are going to behave."

So there it was, the dreaded threat, spoken out loud, shouted in fact, in temper. My heart beat fast. I must placate him. I just pleaded for more time, assuring him my feelings towards him hadn't changed. He went on:

"It's your cousin who has turned you against me. I will get my revenge."

For the rest of that walk I coaxed and cajoled, allowing him to kiss me passionately. I even asked him to take me out for another walk soon; it was so nice to be out with him:

"But now I'm so tired; after all, it's my first time out, and I'd like to go back, please."

I told Diana of the tremendous struggle, and we agreed it would just have to be played by ear – but the stakes were terrifying.

Soon after that I met some of Michel Caldague's friends, the Des Moutis brothers, Patrice and Gilbert. Gilbert was the same age as me and had been at school in Paris for the past four years. The family were very pro-British and, though Gilbert was too young to have belonged to a Résistance group, he and his brother made their own individualistic contribution. Occasionally at night they would bicycle down by the Seine. If there happened to be a couple of German soldiers sauntering along on patrol and no one was in sight, the brothers would quickly shove them into the Seine, boots, greatcoats, rifles and all. Some couldn't swim.

Their elder brother had been killed during the Blitzkrieg, and many of his friends, being older than they, joined the Résistance and were arrested, tortured and shot.

Gilbert was a gentle, charming person and I confided in him. It was ages since I had been able to talk to someone my own age. I told him of my time with the Gestapo and my problem with Karl. He was immensely reassuring and understanding. We played records in the Caldagues' flat – Beethoven's Fifth, very loud. It was the Résistance's theme tune – "*Siffler les V*" . . . dot, dot, dot, dash. We both enjoyed Django Reinhardt, the brilliant guitarist and violinist. It was a most refreshing feeling, to laugh and be normal after my turgid relationship with Karl. Gilbert understood though, and, being the very sweet person he was, could even feel sorry for Karl – in those days.

I still had to go on my *authorized* walks with Karl, but I felt more light-hearted, could pretend more easily, knowing Gilbert and I would soon see each other and I would be able to tell him all about it. Gilbert asked me if I would like to go for a ride. I was hesitant:

132

"I haven't ridden since before the war, and I'm not supposed to leave the flat without Karl."

"Please come. We'll go to the riding school. It will be such fun; no one need know. You can pretend you are still next door and Michel will come with us as chaperone." I couldn't resist it. We didn't tell Diana; it felt like playing truant from school! They had an old mare in a stable near Neuilly, where they lived. She was old and docile and obedient. I cantered gently round the riding school, supremely happy. I was incredibly fond of Gilbert, after only a month, and was afraid I was falling in love with him. I didn't know how he felt about me.

While Michel was having his turn, Gilbert and I sat in an old cab outside. It was the first time we had been alone together. The May sunshine, the delicious smell of stables, made us drunk with happiness. He took my hand and kissed it gently, reverently:

"*Tony, je vous aime, je t'aime eperdument.*" I touched his cheek with my palm, speaking in a whisper, not trusting my voice with the emotion that swept over me:

"*Moi aussi, je t'aime, tu sais.*" We sat there hand in hand, not believing out luck, just looking at each other, lost in each other's eyes and souls. Michel came out and found us:

"It's taken you so long, Gilbert! I thought you'd never dare tell her!" He'd known all along!

It was now physically repulsive to me to be near Karl. He became moody and violent but I still had to see him once or twice a week, in order to avoid reprisals. However, I saw Gilbert every day. On another forbidden outing, he took me to meet his family in Neuilly. They were wonderful, patriotic people, all loathing the Germans. His two sisters were charming and we liked each other from the start. They would listen clandes-

133

BELLINGHAM HIGH SCHOOL LIBRARY

tinely to the B.B.C. and everyone was aware that the Allies were planning something momentous.

Then came 6th June, D-day. It had happened! Excitement in Paris was at fever pitch. The news was patchy, because the B.B.C. stations were jammed. People rushed round in the streets telling everyone they met the latest news. Soon it would all be over – unbelievable. There were rumours that all the water supplies for Paris were going to be blown up, as well as the gas mains and electricity. Diana and I spent a whole day frantically filling empty wine bottles with water, adding one grain of permanganate to each one. We were unaware that the General in charge of Paris, General von Choltitz, was having a bitter struggle with Hitler and the Gestapo. He too loved and appreciated Paris and felt it should be left intact, whereas Hitler wanted to raze it to the ground.

Karl's threats grew worse. He told me that when the Gestapo left Paris, they would take me with them to Germany. Then I would have to marry him.

The rest of June was glorious, making up for the bad weather of the landings. Diana and I prayed and hoped and willed the Allied Armies to succeed in their advance. All over France, Résistance organizations were doing all in their power to help by disrupting communications. For a week or so it had appeared to be touch and go, but now the advance seemed to consolidate. I wondered if my father was with them. Everyone hoped the British would liberate Paris, though that was still a long way off.

Now the Germans started to ransack Paris. As they left in their lorries, they commandeered food, furniture, wine – anything they could lay their hands on. They plundered apartments, hotels and shops. Food became very scarce, and Gilbert and I hitched up the old mare to a cart and drove out of Paris to try and buy potatoes.

Apart from the Germans there was no traffic in Paris, and it was the greatest fun to clip-clop through the streets. We acquired one small sack at an outlandish price!

June drifted into July – one blue, cloudless, hot day after another. In front of an open window in the flat I sunbathed, soaking in the sun and gradually melting the icicles of the winter, the cold, damp cell and all the mental and physical anguish. The sun soon healed the scars on my body and I became really suntanned. Every now and again, if Diana was out playing bridge, I would leave the flat, borrow a bicycle and meet up with Gilbert. We would gleefully pedal among the long columns of German trucks and lorries leaving Paris, covered in branches for camouflage. We would shout insults and sometimes an angry driver would swerve and try and knock one of us down, but bicycles are easily manoeuvrable. Sometimes, too, we would meet in a dimly-lit underground bar in the Rue François 1er. I drank Pernod for the first time, probably the most evocative of all drinks. To this day it conjures up a hot, deliriously excited Paris, the pure unclouded happiness of being, not only in love, but old enough, at eighteen, to know it was real love. I loved Gilbert utterly.

Six weeks after we had met, he asked me to marry him. We were in the Caldagues' flat.

"Tony, I have never loved anyone as I love you, not just because I'm too young to have loved before. But you are unique. I adore you. Please marry me." For the first time I was able to accept with wholehearted joy, not simply because I was either sorry for, or grateful to, or hero-worshipped the person concerned. We had been listening to Django Reinhardt playing "Tea for Two", and this too remains an indelible memory.

The Allies were advancing and the Des Moutis family, along with nearly all the population of Paris, were preparing for the eventual liberation of the city. Despite constant electricity cuts and the appalling shortage of food, Gilbert's sisters were busily sewing Union Jacks and Stars and Stripes on to sheets to hang from the balconies. They asked me how the different crosses should go; shamefacedly, I had to admit I didn't know! The French flag was *so* much simpler!

Gilbert told his family we were engaged and the girls embraced me warmly, thrilled for their brother. The parents must have had reservations, as they would have preferred him to marry a French girl, but they were pleased that he was so happy. (He did marry a French girl many years later, and was very, very happy; so for him all was well.)

While at the dentist, on 20th July, I heard of the attempted assassination of Hitler. It had happened that day. Whispered rumours flew. For the whole of that day no one knew if he had been killed or not. At least it proved without a doubt what a strong anti-Hiler faction existed, not only in the Army, but among the Nazis too.

Diana worried constantly lest something should happen to me. There could only be a few weeks to go before the liberation of Paris. It would be catastrophic if I were whisked off to Germany because of an irate Karl after four and a half years of adventures and near escapes from death. She implored me to be careful, not to go out too often in case Karl should come for me and find me gone. Once again I was being my usual selfish self, with a near-drunken sense of freedom.

Karl did come. He told me the Gestapo was leaving Paris. This was towards the end of July. He was too depressed to be really angry with me:

"Come and say goodbye to me at the hotel before I leave." When he said that, I realized that I was *really* free – free to go out without him. My excitement and joy were hard to conceal from him, though I had to pretend. Just before that last meeting, Gilbert and I had been riding, and I was still in jodhpurs. Gilbert stationed himself near the hotel and said firmly,

"If you don't come out after half an hour, I shall come and fetch you. I have my small revolver with me." I pleaded with him:

"No. Please don't do anything like that. He doesn't know about you. He might be capable of shooting us both, should he find out. He always carries a gun." I reassured Gilbert as best as I could: "I can deal with it."

But my heart was in my mouth, my mouth was dry, and I was trembling all over. Why had I agreed to say goodbye to him there, in his hotel? The answer was simple. It would appear completely genuine, as though I had nothing to hide.

Karl's misery was abject and total. His love for me was sincere, which was why he was leaving me behind in Paris, so that I would be reunited with my parents. I told him I knew how grateful my parents would be to him for saving me from being shot. (I was never able to tell my father the full story. The subject always upset him too much.) I never saw Karl again. But when, a year or so later, and I was in the W.R.N.S., M.I. 5 or 6 interrogated me on my time in the hands of the Gestapo, I spoke up very strongly for him, asking that his behaviour towards me be taken into account. At that time I could remember the name of the "Chief" in Room 333 and utterly condemned his behaviour. I never knew what became of either. I also praised the secretaries in the Gestapo for their clemency towards me. As I knew nothing of the Trepper organization at the time of my questioning by M.I. 5 or 6, I was still no wiser as to the reason for my long imprisonment in the Rue des Saussaies. I could tell them no more than I had told the Gestapo – to wit, Claude Spaak had asked me to write a letter for a friend who needed to go into hiding. They wanted the names of any Gestapo officials I could remember and I was only able to give them two.

Karl kissed me a sad farewell. I ran out of the building, to where Gilbert was waiting in a terrible state. Now I was completely free – no more Karl to be frightened of. No more Gestapo! We bicycled to the quiet little bar in the Rue François 1er and had a drink to celebrate. We could now be together as often as we liked. It was hard to take in. We sat, holding hands, while the pianist played Edith Piaf songs. We said nothing, while I slowly relaxed, unwound and stopped trembling. It was possibly the zenith of happiness. As yet, no other worries had intruded. Life was gloriously simple. We loved each other deeply and we were free, after four years of living in real fear. We had less than a month to be together; it was lucky we could not have foreseen that.

The battle seemed to be a long time reaching Paris. Everyone still hoped that the British would be allowed to liberate Paris with the Americans, but it seemed unlikely. German troops still held Paris and were installed in the key positions. If you have seen the film or read the book, *Is Paris Burning?* you will know what it was like when Paris was liberated, mainly by its own Résistance forces.

In mid-August the sound of the big guns could be heard in the distance – the most exhilarating sound you could wish to hear. There had also been some pinpoint bombing by the R.A.F. of strategic communications and ammunition centres. In that final week fighting erupted all over Paris. There was a strict curfew imposed from 7 p.m. to 7 a.m. to safeguard civilians.

The ordinary citizens were unaware of the confrontation between von Choltitz, the General commanding

Paris who wished to preserve it, and Jodl, the Nazi General, who, with Hitler, wanted to flatten Paris. The F.F.I. (*Forces Françaises de l'Intérieur*) and the various Resistance groups had waited five long years for this momentous week.

Gilbert had helped to put up barbed-wire entanglements to hinder the Germans left defending Paris. He also had a small pistol and an armband which showed him to be a member of the Résistance. He helped where he could. No one knew that explosives were being laid under the bridges of Paris, under the Chamber of Deputies and other beautiful buildings. Hitler was beside himself with fury at losing Paris to a largely unarmed collection of fighting men. He ordered two S.S. Panzer Divisions to go back to Paris and raze it to the ground. Fortunately they were too busy elsewhere!

At the time it all seemed a heady, exciting muddle. Despite Diana's warning, I couldn't resist going out with Gilbert. We slid along the buildings, hiding in doorways as shots were fired in the streets. We bought Diana a big bunch of flowers as a peace-offering. Quite rightly, she was furious and not appeased by the flowers!

One evening, after Gilbert had been to see me, he missed the curfew by a few minutes, and he knew his mother would be desperately worried. The telephones were not working. Michel Caldagues reassured him:

"I'll bicycle with you some of the way. Its only just after 7 p.m. We'll be all right." They set off, pedalling furiously. After about five or ten minutes I heard shots, very close and distinct. It was usually quiet after curfew. I waited in great anxiety. Michel arrived back alone, with a horrifying tale. They had reached the end of the street at the bottom of the Rue Casimir Périer and had been stopped by Germans, ordering them off their bicycles. Gilbert had ordered Michel to turn tail and zig-zag back, while he distracted the soldiers. When he had looked back for a glimpse of Gilbert, it was to see him standing against a wall and the Germans raising their rifles. Michel was in despair, and so was I. There was nothing we could do. The night seemed endless. At 7 a.m. I went out into the street, not caring what happened. My feet and heart seemed made of lead. I thought I must be dreaming when I saw a tall figure in blue shorts appear round the corner! It was Gilbert – alive. I ran to him, tears of relief streaming down my cheeks.

"What happened?" He told me. The German patrol had put his bicycle in their lorry and then lined him up against the wall to be shot. He didn't even think, he just acted. He was *not* going to stand and be shot in cold blood, so he set off at a tremendous pace, zig-zagging, while the Germans ran behind him, shooting. He was faster than them and, having rounded a corner, he dived into a block of flats and up the stairs. He pounded on the door of the first floor, but no one answered. With lungs bursting and the shouts of the Germans ominously closer, he tore up to the second floor. There someone let him in and put him in a bed, well covered up. When the Germans reached the door soon after, demanding to be let in, the man opened it, with a finger on his lips, asking them to be very quiet, as his son was very ill with scarlet fever.

"Have you seen anyone dashing up the stairs?"

"No; but I heard shooting, and when I looked out of the window I glimpsed a young man in shorts running very fast." His presence of mind saved Gilbert's life. Any hesitation in his story would have been fatal. The whole incident only took a few moments. (Shortly after my return, I broadcast this episode on the B.B.C. in the

"French for Schools" programme. The broadcast was arranged by my mother who was anxious for me to get a job with the B.B.C.)

What an incredible escape! He took me to see the marks the bullets had made in the walls – fresh, white, chipped scars. They were still there a few years later.

Next day was the day of the battle for the Chambre des Députés. As it was so close to the flat, it sounded horrendous. The Germans had got a big anti-tank gun mounted in the courtyard and were told to defend the building to the last man. A comparative silence fell, followed by the rumbling of tanks and wild cheering. Gilbert and I went down into the street, and there were General Le Clerc's tanks and men, all gloriously mixed up with the F.F.I. in ragged clothes and armbands. The Square was packed with people singing the *Marseillaise*, crying, cheering and embracing each other. The battle was still going on spasmodically. We joined in. Then they started bringing the German wounded out of the Chambre des Députés – some walking, some on stretchers. The French were revengeful and full of loathing. They forced a way to the wounded men and actually spat on them. I was horrified. I could feel nothing but pity for the poor soldiers who had only been obeying orders. British people would not have behaved like that, I felt. Odd shots were still being fired from isolated pockets and snipers on the roofs. We went back to the flat to tell Diana about it. That same day, and the next, groups of shaven French women and men, hands on their heads, were being marched down the streets. These were the collaborators, so-called. The crowd spat on them too. Again I wondered if such behaviour would occur in similar circumstances in England.

The bells rang out all over Paris. The Église Sainte Clothilde was opposite No. 17 and the ringing epitomized what a whole nation was feeling – the joy of freedom from nightmarish oppression.

No one went to bed that night. All Paris was celebrating. The lights were switched on for that one night. The next morning the first Americans drove down the Rue Casimir Périer. I saw them from the window and tore down to welcome them. They hauled me up on their tank and I greeted them in my rather bad English, shaking hands with them all. They cheerfully commented:

"Your English sure ain't very good, but we reckon you're not French, or you'd have kissed us!"

"Want a ride?" they chorused. An open jeep had drawn up alongside, and a young officer asked me if I knew the way to such and such a street.

"That would be wonderful!" I shouted. "Yes, I know where the street is." Off we went on a hair-raising drive round Paris, firmly going the wrong way round the entire Place de la Concorde. The spontaneous happiness of those madcap days of liberation cannot be fully understood by those who had not experienced the occupation. It was bubbling and infectious, like a continuous draught of vintage champagne.

I had forgotten all about Peter Dougall. But of course, as soon as St. Denis was freed, all the British internees poured out. He must have got my address from his sister Jean. This was an unforeseen problem. Gilbert, endlessly understanding and kind, told me,

"That poor boy, he's been shut up for nearly five years. You must see him, and don't break it to him straight away that we are engaged."

When he came to the flat, I hardly recognized him. He had changed from a boy to a man and had imagined himself engaged to me all this time. I could not bring myself to tell him. He kissed me hungrily and I wondered how he had learned to kiss like that in prison – it was only a peck on the cheek accompanied by blushes when I had last seen him. He too was savouring the ecstasy of freedom.

"Don't let's talk about the things that have happened to us; let's just be happy today and revel in it," he begged. I seemed fated to have to deceive. How he became aware of the change in me, I never knew. Maybe Diana dealt with it. I don't think I saw him again. The idea uppermost in his mind was to get back to England and join the R.A.F. before the war was over. He did, and was killed.

De Gaulle was due to march down the Champs Elysées in a Victory Parade with some of his Generals, Juin being possibly the most famous. The Héry's office was on the Champs Elysées and Diana was invited to watch it from there. Gilbert and I went on our bicycles; we wanted to be part of the crowd on the ground. The cheering from the hundreds of thousands of people all shouting "*Vive de Gaulle*" was deafening. He was unmistakable – so tall and dignified and apparently unmoved as he walked slowly down the Avenue flanked by his officers. As he passed, all the crowd surged behind him. Tears of pride and joy were in everyone's eyes. After all, he and Churchill had been a constant inspiration and source of strength throughout the war. We shouted ourselves hoarse. It was an apotheosis never to be repeated, never to be forgotten, a unique enshrined emotion.

We hardly heard the first sniper's shots which rang out. De Gaulle and his entourage never flinched. Some of the onlookers rushed into doorways, looking up at the windows and roofs opposite. We jumped on our bicyces and decided to ride back to the flat via the Place des Invalides. There were very few people there, and as we rode past the old cannons outside the Invalides more shots rang out.

"*Mon Dieu! Ils nous tirent dessus.*" We threw ourselves to the ground and hid under the bicycles. Their protection seemed ludicrously inadequate and the Place des Invalides seemed immense. It was funny remembering that incident seventeen years later when I showed my English sons Napoleon's tomb.

When the shooting had died down we rode back to the flat. Diana, in the office, had not fared much better. The shooting was coming from opposite at that point, and they all had to throw themselves on the floor.

Less than a week later there was a telephone call – from Brigadier Lyon-Smith. It was unbelievable. His voice sounded just the same. He was C.R.A. of the 7th Armoured Division, well to the north of Paris unfortunately, but as soon as a lull in the battle permitted he would drive down in his jeep to see us. He told us,

"The Huns are retreating so fast we can hardly keep up with them!" Diana and I shared the call, too moved to say much.

Of course my one idea was to introduce Gilbert to my father. Sadly, amidst the welter of excitement, I knew how desperately heartbroken I would be to leave my beloved France. I had lived through so much with her, grown up, loved, nearly died with her. And still, thirty-three years later, I feel the same.

There was a ring at the door. I opened it and there, resplendent in his uniform, stood my father. After a quick hug, he took one look at me and said,

"What *have* you done to your hair, all piled up on top like that? Comb it down. And take off those ridiculous shoes!" They were wooden-soled and wedge-shaped and made me taller than my father! The laughter eased the unbearable emotion of seeing each other again after nearly five years. He could only stay one night. The battle wouldn't wait for him. But he promised to arrange for me to fly home as soon as possible. I drove with him in his jeep to where I had arranged to meet Gilbert, and introduced them. I could sense that my father disapproved strongly of my becoming engaged to a Frenchman. He had not got a very high opinion of the French. Also he was desperately tired. His war had been gruelling – British Expeditionary Force, North Africa, then the landings – and it was by no means finished. We both drove with him to the north of Paris where we said goodbye. Then he drove back to the war and we caught a Metro back to Paris.

I felt I should be thrilled at the thought of going back to England to see my mother. But, as the days passed, the dread and unhappiness Gilbert and I felt leaving each other outweighed any other feelings.

An Army Padre came to see Diana and me. He had been asked to "get me back somehow". This had been carefully organized. I was to fly in a Red Cross plane, carrying medical supplies to a front-line hospital camp, and from there wait for transport back to England. I had no passport. My only means of identification was a signed letter from my father, with an official "7th Armoured Division" stamp on it in red, merely stating that I was his daughter and should be given all possible help in repatriating me to England.

Gilbert and I were heartbroken at parting. We swore to write to each other daily, and this we did for a year. But my mother did not want me to marry a Frenchman and I did not see him again for a quarter of a century.

The big military 'plane landed me and my small suitcase at a front-line hospital under canvas. There were hundreds of tents. I was taken to one which I was to share with three nursing sisters. They looked curiously at me, and admittedly I must have looked very foreign, with my old ski-boots and my hair piled high. My English was appalling and I couldn't follow their conversation or understand half of what they said. I felt as though I had been wafted on to another planet. To them I was a nuisance. I thought they were quite wonderful and admired without reserve their cool, calm attitude. My admiration knew no bounds when one of them, at a mealtime, said:

"You'll see, [this to the other nurses, I was completely ignored] no sooner will we have put the theatre up than we'll be off again, following the advance." I really thought they were going to put on a show for the wounded. How could they possibly find time with all the nursing? "Theatre" only had one meaning for me. Thank goodness I never opened my mouth more than was strictly necessary.

I was there for two or thee days, eating heartily of the delicious food. During the last few months in Paris we had been on semi-starvation diet.

Then I was taken to a small airfield where a Mosquito stood waiting. This was most exciting – real V.I.P. treatment. A pilot and a navigator all to myself! The plane was bare, and all I had to sit on was what resembled a tractor seat. They flew low over Caen to show me the damage, but I was already feeling air-sick! They then had to follow certain "safe" air corridors, and the flight took hours. The men jokingly told me there was nowhere for me to be sick anyway.

"Oh, look! There are the white cliffs of Dover; bet it's a long time since you saw them!" But I felt too sick to care what happened or where we were. I couldn't even sleep because I would have fallen off the bucket seat, which had no back or arms!

Finally, bruised and tired, we landed at Northolt. A horde of officials descended on us, with a "You can't land there, you know" look. Somehow I had expected a *warm* welcome – not a *hero's* welcome but just a "Nice to have you back in England again" welcome.

Not a bit of it. I was treated like a spy! I produced my father's letter and they went into a huddle and marched me off to an office. I thought that at any moment they would put me in prison! They interrogated me closely for two hours. When I asked if I could telephone my mother in Scotland, they shuddered as though I had committed an act of treason and flatly refused. I tried to reason with them. After all, they were English, my own kind, on my side.

"Surely, if I *was* a spy, I would have had a bona fide passport and wouldn't have landed quite so conspicuously!" This remark shocked and annoyed them so much that I kept quiet.

No transport was provided for me and by the time I was told to go I was in tears.

"Go where? And how? I don't know where I am. I don't know London, and I want to go to Scotland."

"Oh! you've missed the night train now. I should go to the station and wait around there." Perhaps you won't believe this, but in fact it is a watered-down version of my reception. How I longed to go back to France, already.

They pointed me in the direction of an underground station. I was carrying my own suitcase and it was nearly dark by now. I asked someone how to use the telephone, and a kind stranger rang the Ayrshire number for me. The sound of my mother's voice renewed my tears. I told her I was going to sit on the platform till the morning train up to Glasgow, but she insisted on my going to the station hotel. It was the time of the V.1.s or V.2.s, so London was pretty empty.

When I asked the receptionist for a room, looking and sounding so foreign, she was about to say "No" when in desperation I blurted out,

"Please. I've just flown back from France, after four years." I didn't realize how unusual this was. The girl actually smiled and said,

"Yes, would you like a room with a bath?"

"Yes, please, I haven't had one for four years!" I could only have one a few inches deep, but it felt like utter luxury.

At breakfast I was astounded to find a woman in fancy dress at the table. It was a W.R.N.S. officer, but I had never even heard of the women's services. I merely thought.

"What a mad country, but no doubt the French seem mad to them." The joy of eating marmalade, after the same time-gap as the baths, made up for a lot.

Eventually, very travel weary and lost, I reached Glasgow in the dark. I wandered up and down the platform searching for my mother. We must have passed each other several times in the gloom unable to recognize each other. She was in W.V.S. uniform and much smaller than I remembered her. Finally we were the only two left on the platform.

PUBLISHER'S NOTE

Many readers may wish to know a little bit about what happened to Antonia after her momentous adventures. Immediately, of course, after they had met at the station, Antonia and her mother had a great deal of catching up to do, not to mention getting to know each other again. Antonia's mother was living in an hotel near Ayr and they both went back there for what one might call a debriefing. Alas, a great many of the guests in the hotel insisted on pestering poor Antonia with questions over the following few days. At first she tried to answer them and describe and explain what she had been through. It quickly became apparent to her that no one believed her. To them it sounded like "Propaganda". To be fair it should be remembered that it was still 1944 and not much first-hand information had yet filtered out of occupied Europe. Quite what Antonia's mother thought about the whole thing must go unrecorded.

After six months Antonia had sufficiently recovered to join one of the Women's Services and she duly enrolled in the W.R.N.S. which she says quickly restored her to normality and she began to enjoy her life as a signaller.

Her mother had strong ideas about her future and did not wish Antonia to marry a Frenchman, so after a "heart-breaking" year the engagement was broken off. Instead, Antonia married a Naval Officer, a submariner and they bought an old R.N.L.I. lifeboat. Her next few years were spent sailing round the coast of England to France and Holland. Also during this time two children were born. Antonia is now writing another book about this part of her life which she says will be more lighthearted than this one.

She now lives with her second husband and their son in a beautiful cottage in Devon – a cottage which her publisher attempts to visit as often as possible since the catering is three star and the conversation likewise.

The memories of those early years live on though and who would be surprised at that after reading this remarkable book.

L.C.